CREEPIEST PLACES ON EARTH

NAHANNI VALLEY
Aka Headless Valley

Timothy D.
Field Researcher & Author

CREEPIEST PLACES ON EARTH

Nahanni Valley: Aka Headless Valley

© 2025 Timothy D.

All rights reserved.

No part of this publication may be reproduced, distributed, or transmitted in any form or by any means, including photocopying, recording, or other electronic or mechanical methods, without the prior written permission of the author, except in the case of brief quotations used in critical reviews or scholarly analysis.

ISBN: 978-1-0691212-3-3
First Edition, 2025

Cover design by Timothy D.

This is a work of nonfiction. All efforts have been made to verify the details, but some names or locations may be altered for privacy or narrative purposes. The author accepts no responsibility for the reader's interpretation of the material within.

Preface

One of the Creepiest Places on Earth-Nahanni Valley

Hidden deep within the Mackenzie Mountains of the Northwest Territories, not far from the Yukon border, lies one of the most remote and mysterious wildernesses on the continent: Nahanni National Park Reserve of Canada.

Spanning over 30,000 square kilometers, this isolated region is carved by the South Nahanni River, a powerful waterway flanked by towering canyons and roaring with the thunder of Virginia Falls, twice the height of Niagara. Recognized as a UNESCO World Heritage Site since 1978, Nahanni is a landscape of raw beauty — and unresolved danger.

What makes this place truly infamous, however, is not just the geography. It's the growing list of strange and chilling events tied to it.

Beginning in the early 20th century, stories of gold prospectors found dead — some decapitated, others vanished entirely — ignited a mystery that never quite burned out. Most famously, in 1908, brothers Willie and Frank McLeod disappeared, only to be discovered years later as headless skeletons near the riverbank. Over forty such cases have since been recorded. None with satisfying answers.

But the stories stretch further back. Dene and other First Nations peoples have long warned of the valley's dangers, describing it as a "forbidden place," said to be guarded by spirits, giants, or beings unseen. Modern explorers and backcountry guides speak of Sasquatch-like creatures, glowing orbs, prehistoric shapes moving through the mists, and hot springs that steam in winter without freezing — all adding to Nahanni's surreal atmosphere.

You can't drive into Nahanni. You must fly in by floatplane or paddle upriver through fast water and unmarked terrain. That inaccessibility only fuels its reputation — a place few visit, and fewer understand.

Some come seeking wilderness. Others come chasing legends.

But everyone who leaves agrees:

This is one of the creepiest places on Earth.

Table Of Contents

Preface
Prologue – The Map That Didn't Fit

Chapter 1 – Headless and Unsolved
Chapter 2 – Fire as a Signature
Chapter 3 – The Valley That Eats Maps
Chapter 4 – The Curve
Chapter 5 – The Ones Who Got Close
Chapter 6 – The Animals Don't Go There
Chapter 7 – The Uncounted
Chapter 8 – Things Found That Shouldn't Be
Chapter 9 – The River Remembers
Chapter 10 – Witnesses Who Lied
Chapter 11 – Fire Doesn't Behave Here
Chapter 12 – The Ridge No One Climbs
Chapter 13 – The Creek That Changed Direction
Chapter 14 – The Room with No Walls
Chapter 15 – Patterns in the Bone Dust
Chapter 16 – The Ice Doesn't Keep Them
Chapter 17 – They Carried Something Back
Chapter 18 – The Ones Who Stayed
Chapter 19 – If You Hear Your Name
Chapter 20 – The Last Map Doesn't Match
Chapter 21 – Shadow at Noon
Chapter 22 – The Sound the Ground Makes
Chapter 23 – The Ones Who Drew Maps Too Late
Chapter 24 – The Disappearances That Rewrote the Timeline
Chapter 25 – The Things That Left No Footprints
Chapter 26 – The Ones Who Heard the Singing
Chapter 27 – The Quiet Between the Pines
Chapter 28 – They Never Found Their Own Camps
Chapter 29 – They Came Back Changed
Chapter 30 – They Built Fires for the Wrong Reasons
Chapter 31 – The Coordinates You Shouldn't Say Out Loud
Chapter 32 – What the Birds Refuse to Fly Over
Chapter 33 – The Ledge That Isn't On the Map
Chapter 34 – The Trail Markers That Change
Chapter 35 – When the Maps Disagree with the Ground
Chapter 36 – The Tribe That Walked Into the Valley
Chapter 37 – The Mammoth Trail and the Warm Ground
Chapter 38 – They Left Notes They Didn't Write
Chapter 39 – When the Silence Starts to Follow You
Chapter 40 – The Fires That No One Claimed
Chapter 41 – The Camps Found with Everything But the People

Chapter 42 – They Marked Trees That Were Already Marked
Chapter 43 – The Warnings in the Wind
Chapter 45 – The Screaming That Wasn't Heard By Everyone
Chapter 46 – The Lights That Don't Illuminate
Chapter 47 – The Tracks That Went Up the Cliff Face
Chapter 48 – The Path That Wasn't on the Satellite Image Yesterday
Chapter 49 – The Trees That Don't Fall the Right Way
Chapter 50 – The Day the Compass Pointed Up
Chapter 51 – The Whisper Caves
Chapter 52 – The Camps That Were Too New
Chapter 53 – The Ones Who Slept Too Long
Chapter 54 – When the Radios Played Back Their Own Words
Chapter 55 – The Ridge Where Drones Fail
Chapter 56 – The Skeletons That Didn't Belong to Anything
Chapter 57 – The Ice That Burned
Chapter 58 – The Season That Loops
Chapter 59 – The Campfires Already Burning
Chapter 60 – The Hills That Hum at Dusk
Chapter 61 – The Ones Who Watched from the Trees
Chapter 62 – The Creatures That Shouldn't Still Be Here
Chapter 63 – What the Valley Keeps

Appendix A – Cryptid Encounter Log: Nahanni Non-Hominid Sightings
Appendix B – Master Log of Unexplained Phenomena in the Nahanni Valley
Appendix C – Indigenous Lore & Place-Name Interpretations
Appendix D – Map of Nahanni

Prologue – The Map That Didn't Fit

It started with a map I shouldn't have trusted. Not because it was fake—but because it was real in a way that didn't make sense. The contour lines were right. The river paths mostly aligned. But there was something off about the spacing, the way distances didn't scale, the way one valley curve repeated in two places half a kilometer apart. I stared at that loop for days before realizing it wasn't a printing error. Someone had drawn it like that. Not just on this one copy, but on others I found tucked in ranger logs, aviation charts, even a black-and-white fax buried in an old geological survey from 1983. I tried to trace the source of the inconsistency. Who marked it, why it stuck. That led me to five missing person cases—four confirmed, one presumed. All within the same elliptical bend in the South Nahanni River. And all over a thirty-year span. No patterns. No witnesses. No recoveries. Only clues, and even those felt reluctant.

The Nahanni has always had a reputation. Some call it the Valley of Headless Men. Others, the Place That Watches. Legends talk about fireballs above the spruce line, figures seen at the edges of camps, voices under the wind. I'd heard the stories, but I didn't chase folklore. I chased what remained. Boots found near tree lines. Knife sheaths left on boulders with no blood, no struggle. Campfires burned inward. Equipment that stopped working and stayed broken until you left the valley. Things the RCMP called tragic. Things the locals called old. And somewhere in that tangled narrative—caught between satellite imagery and stories told over AM radio—was this map. This bend. This place that didn't want to stay where it was drawn.

I hadn't planned to write about Nahanni. I had been working cases from Ontario to Montana, tracing weird disappearances and long-term search failures. But the deeper I fell into this valley's history, the more it pulled back. I submitted Freedom of Information requests and got responses so heavily redacted they looked more like Morse code. I found entries from old fire watch towers referencing "ground dissonance" and "aural doubling." And then there was the tape—a DAT archive labeled FIELD_RAV_97_21. The voice on it was steady, clipped, male. He repeated coordinates, weather data, timestamps. But then, just before the audio cuts, he says it: "...object submerged under southern bend... watching from below." That's all. No name. No conclusion. Just that voice, and the rising white noise behind it.

I'm not here to convince anyone of anything. What you believe about this place isn't my concern. I'm not here to debunk, and I'm not here to evangelize. I'm here because the story demanded it. Because the valley kept appearing in documents where it didn't belong, and because when I tried to turn away from it—my maps started changing. Digitally. Physically. One even reprinted itself with the curve twice. I don't know how. But I took that as a sign. And I booked the flight.

This book is the record of everything that came before I stepped onto the floatplane. What I found. What I didn't. The patterns in the fog. The shadows on the paper. The stories others tried not to tell. And the ones I had to pry loose. I spent two years chasing a curve that won't hold still. Now I have five days inside it.

And maybe, if I listen hard enough, I'll learn why the map didn't fit.

Chapter 1 – Headless and Unsolved

They were found with their heads missing. That's how it starts. That's how it always starts when you talk about Nahanni. The McLeod brothers—Martin and Willie—left Edmonton in 1906 to find gold rumored to rival Klondike. They headed up the South Nahanni River with supplies, rifles, and a dog that never made it back. They didn't either. A year later, another party came through and found their bodies near Flat River. Their heads were gone. Cleanly removed. Not by animals. Not by time. One of them was still clutching a loaded rifle. There were no signs of a fight. Their gear was untouched. No gold, but that's not what stuck in the official report. What stuck was the way their bodies were found—intentional, careful, emptied of identity.

Some say it was the Dene people, guarding sacred land. But the Dene don't decapitate. And they're not shy about naming what they protect. Others said it was rival prospectors, but nothing was stolen. Just the heads. Just the names.

It wasn't an isolated case.

In 1917, a trapper's camp was found abandoned. A pot still boiling over the fire. Meat hanging. Rifle propped beside the bedroll. Everything in place. But the trapper was gone. His name was never written down, only passed between lodge meetings and local supply stations. Then in 1946, a prospector named Albert Lamb went missing. Same area. Same outcome. His camp was found undisturbed. His tools still neatly stacked in a canvas roll. No signs of panic. No bear prints. No drag marks. No blood.

The RCMP files from that period are thin. Paper fades. Names get misfiled. One logbook lists "Subject likely drowned; extreme terrain." But locals whisper something else: that the land doesn't give back what it takes.

I started requesting records. Some came clean. Most were redacted—names blacked out, coordinates missing, entire paragraphs labeled "Lost in archival transit." When I called a Parks Canada contact, she paused for five seconds before saying, "You're asking about Nahanni?" Not the case. Not the year. Just the place. Like that was enough.

What makes this so difficult to track isn't the silence—it's the repetition. It happens again and again. The same vanishings. The same locations. Slight variations on the same impossible outcomes. Camps left intact. Weapons unfired. Packs zipped. Radios working but never used.

One RCMP case from 1981—B. Kearns and M. Dupree—reads like a modern echo of the McLeod brothers. They were experienced hikers. Had filed an itinerary. They made it past Rabbitkettle Lake. Then nothing. Their tent was found weeks later. Zipped shut from the inside.

No damage. No blood. Their food was untouched. Compass found spinning in place—magnetic interference unexplained.

In the records, you can feel the bureaucratic shrug behind the language. "Presumed hypothermia." "Voluntary disappearance." "Possible animal predation." But you don't take your gear off in the cold. You don't wander unarmed with your tent zipped behind you. You don't disappear silently in a straight-line valley where voices echo for miles.

Somewhere between 1908 and now, Nahanni stopped being a gold rush mystery and started being something else. Something quieter. Smarter. It doesn't chase. It waits. You don't stumble into it. You pass through it and don't come out. And it's not interested in witnesses. Only absence.

The deeper I went into the files, the more one pattern emerged: **no confirmed eyewitnesses. Not once.** Not in a hundred years. Only recovery parties. Only second-hand sightings. Or worse—beacons that stop mid-transmission. Radios that cut off. A final photograph showing nothing out of place, followed by a decade of silence.

Nahanni eats stories the same way it eats people: completely, and without evidence.

Chapter 2 – Fire as a Signature

There are places in the Nahanni where the ground shouldn't burn—but does. Places where moss and permafrost exist side by side, and yet someone—or something—has left scorch marks. Not the kind caused by a careless campfire. Not lightning. Not even wildfire. These are precise. Circular. Clean. And wrong.

The first one I found wasn't in an official record. It was a passing line in a 1955 ranger field journal archived in Yellowknife: "Found burn patch east of Rabbitkettle. 12-foot ring. No tree damage. No smell." That was it. No investigation. No photographs. Just a sentence written like it was better left that way.

The phenomenon repeats. A hunter's map from 1978, now housed in a private collection, has a circle marked in red pencil with a single word: "glassed." Soil samples taken from a site near Virginia Falls in 1987—now declassified from a university research grant—show traces of silica vitrification. That's what happens when sand turns to glass under extreme heat. The kind of heat measured at over 1700 degrees Celsius. But this wasn't near a volcano, a firepit, or a lightning scar. It was in the center of a mossy clearing. Everything within a 10-foot radius: sterilized. Outside that? Untouched.

In one case, a burn was found deep within a slot canyon where no natural ignition source could have reached. A climber flagged it with a drone—thermal signature peaking 60°C above surrounding rock temperature. The drone failed mid-scan. Its storage card came back scrambled. The pilot logged it, then refused to return.

I catalogued 14 verified cases and nearly double that in undocumented whispers. The sites are scattered, but not randomly. They align to a path that almost forms a spiral—broad, then tightening. Each occurrence gets more precise. More controlled. None of these were reported in connection with disappearances. But five overlap within two kilometers of known missing-person events.

When I uploaded the data into my pattern recognition engine, the results were flagged anomalous. Too much heat. Too little spread. Inconsistent thermal decay. "Signature not consistent with any known natural wildfire or anthropogenic ignition," the model reported. It even assigned an uncertainty variable: *intentional burn without source*.

The cases are made stranger by the absence of traditional fire behavior. No charring up tree trunks. No animal displacement. No lingering smell of smoke. Just scorched earth. And sometimes, strange remnants. In one photo—retrieved from an anonymous upload in a climber's forum—something metallic sits half-submerged in the soil. Melted around the edges. No one ever came forward to identify it.

Locals are reluctant to talk. But the few who do repeat an old Dene phrase that roughly translates to, *"Fire is the land's way of saying no."* Not as a warning. As a verdict.

Not every mystery is about vanishing. Some are about what's left behind.

Burns in Nahanni are not accidents. They are punctuation marks.

And the story they're ending… hasn't finished yet.

Chapter 3 – The Valley That Eats Maps

Maps are supposed to work. Especially now. We live in a world of satellites, GIS overlays, digital topography, LIDAR scans. You can measure the curvature of a planet from orbit, yet Nahanni still eats maps.

It started subtle. A grid mismatch in a 1977 aviation chart. A ridge that shouldn't have been there. Contour lines that doubled back and disappeared. It was attributed to aging print plates. Then came the GPS anomalies: one hiker recorded himself walking due north and ended up due west. Another reported elevation gain on perfectly flat terrain. These were dismissed—user error, outdated units, poor sky coverage. But the reports kept coming.

In 2004, a Parks Canada field team noted that their digital topo maps wouldn't sync with handheld GPS units. Coordinates drifted, then snapped back. At one point, they marked a flagged tree. An hour later, it was gone. Then reappeared behind them. They logged it as "data latency." That was the official term.

But there's no lag in the human eye.

One researcher compared LIDAR scans taken five years apart. The terrain shifted. Not drastically—just enough. One ridgeline grew steeper. A dry basin filled with topographic noise. Elevation markers blinked out. The software marked it as "data redundancy loss." But the redundancy was human: two analysts seeing something that wasn't supposed to be there... and agreeing on it.

The more I collected maps, the more they argued with each other. One ranger map from 1993 shows a canyon that doesn't appear on any satellite data. A 1981 climber's guide has notations of a "false gulch"—a kind of shadow ravine that appears on foot but disappears on camera. Even the Dene elders refer to "land that forgets itself."

In one case, a bush pilot flying a familiar supply route had to circle twice. The river had moved. Not flooded. Not swollen. Moved. He marked it, and returned the next week to find it where it should've been all along.

I brought the data into the AI model. Plotted all known map discrepancies from 1950 to now. It didn't give me a clear cause. Just a phrase in the diagnostic margin: **"non-persistent terrain alignment"** — followed by this:
"Warning: Source terrain is unstable in a cartographic context. Recommend analog navigation only."

I stared at that line for ten minutes.

This isn't about poor maps. This is about a landscape that **resists documentation**. A place that un-makes itself in subtle, quiet ways. That bends just enough to undo your sense of where you were—so that when something goes wrong, you're not even sure where to look for answers. Or bodies.

People think getting lost is about taking a wrong turn. In Nahanni, it might be about turning and finding the path itself is gone.

That's not just dangerous. That's deliberate.

The only consistent way through this place, I'm beginning to realize, is **memory**. And even that… has seams in it.

Chapter 4 – The Curve

They don't name it on maps. It's just a bend in the river—one of dozens. But everyone I interviewed who had been to the area, or near it, or *almost* there, referred to it the same way: **The Curve**. Capital C. Like a landmark no one wants to talk about directly, but everyone understands.

On topographic charts, it's an elegant oxbow near the southern arm of the South Nahanni River. But when you overlay incident reports—confirmed disappearances, thermal anomalies, GPS failures, and "unexplained retreat logs"—it becomes something else entirely. A clustering node. A dead zone of coincidence.

The first flagged disappearance near The Curve was in 1946—Albert Lamb. I already mentioned him. But it wasn't until 1981 that someone officially noted the geographic overlap. A Parks Canada search log scrawled a line in the margin: *"Again—south of the bend."* That phrase is now burned into my research notes. Not because of what it says—but because of what it implies. *They knew it before they understood it.*

I contacted the cartographer who helped digitize the terrain scans in 2009. He remembered The Curve without prompting. "There was something off with the reflectivity," he said. "The LIDAR showed a shimmer—like an echo on the ground." When I asked what that meant, he paused. "You know how sonar pings? We got something like that. But from *land*."

I've spoken to two bush pilots who refuse to fly over it. One said the air gets "soft." That was his word. Not turbulence. Not wind shear. *Soft*. "Like the wings float different." He went silent when I pressed him. Said he was tired. Didn't call back.

The Dene don't name it. That's important. They name everything else—every ridge, valley, stream, pass. But when asked, they just point on the map and say, *"There."* No story. No myth. Just avoidance.

In my AI pattern model, The Curve sits at the convergence of multiple flagged zones: topographic distortion, flora anomalies, signal interference, and elevation mismatches. It's the only location that scored in every anomaly category. The AI labeled it a "high-weight anomaly zone" and advised a physical investigation. That recommendation felt more like a dare.

And so, I've planned my entry. The Curve is where I'll make my first major inland camp. Not nearby. Not observing. Inside. I'll cross the bend. Set up in its belly. And wait.

Somewhere in that land, the truth isn't just buried—it's *folded*. Like the terrain remembers differently. Like the valley itself has a memory… and forgets selectively.

I don't know what I'll find there.

But I'm not going in blind.

Chapter 5 – The Ones Who Got Close

There aren't many who've come back. That's what makes these cases stand out. Not because they survived — but because something about them didn't.

In 1972, a geology student named Fred Bower was part of a summer survey crew sent into the Ragged Range. His report was clean, scientific, normal — until the final entry:
"Woke up to a high-pitched pulsing. Thought it was tinnitus. Couldn't hear my own breath. Everything felt slow. Like the air had thickened."
The rest of his notes stop. What we know next comes from a medivac request filed by his partner two days later. Bower was found unresponsive, eyes open, hands clenched around a compass that no longer pointed anywhere. He recovered speech after three weeks in Yellowknife. But when asked what happened, he only said: "It showed me a room with no walls."

He never returned to the field.

Case Two: a hunter named Derek Simani in 1998. An experienced tracker, Cree-Métis, with dozens of logged trips under his belt. He entered alone from the west near Tungsten and emerged six days later without his rifle, pack, or boots. He walked into a ranger cabin barefoot. When asked what happened, he didn't speak. Just wrote one word in charcoal on the wall:
"Listening."
He wouldn't explain it. He still won't. He's alive today — lives in Whitecourt, Alberta — but won't give interviews. I wrote him twice. No reply. But someone slid a note under my motel door in Hay River the night after I asked around town.
"He said the trees aren't just trees."

I don't know who left it.

Third case: 2002, anonymous subject. This one never made it into public record — I found it buried in a chain of internal Parks Canada emails during a document pull.
"He walked out. Wouldn't speak. Spent the next year in Yellowknife under psychiatric hold. Refuses to talk about what he saw. Keeps drawing trees with no tops. And eyes."
No name. No report. Just that.
But the drawing matched one I'd seen years earlier, pinned in an abandoned ranger station near the Flat River bend. Same pattern. Same eyes. Same blank sky.

These aren't accidents. These aren't people who got lost and came back shaken. They're people who *saw something* — or got close enough to feel the edge of it — and couldn't explain it in human language. Not trauma. Not madness. Something else. A kind of *lingering echo*.

Every region of high-strangeness has these figures. In UFO folklore they're the "experiencers." In the realm of hauntings, they're the "sensitive ones." But here… here, in Nahanni, they're different. They don't evangelize. They don't speak. They **withdraw**. Like whatever they saw didn't just shock them — it *warned* them.

I plotted their last known coordinates. They form a kind of crescent — flanking, but never entering, a central zone near The Curve. Not one of these individuals crossed the river bend. And not one attempted to return.

That's what links them. Not what they saw.

But that they *knew* not to go any farther.

Chapter 6 – The Animals Don't Go There

The first sign isn't what's present. It's what's *missing*.

Nahanni is rich with life — caribou, moose, wolves, bears, snowshoe hares, lynx. It's a living wilderness. But every account I've collected, every field log, every ranger interview, includes the same eerie note: there are pockets where **nothing moves**. No birds. No tracks. No scat. Not even bugs.

I interviewed a retired wildlife surveyor who worked in the area for over fifteen years. She didn't hesitate when I asked if she ever noticed "dead zones."
"All the time," she said. "Places where your skin itches but there's no mosquitoes. Nothing scatters when you step through brush. No birds overhead. Not even droppings. Just… absence."
I asked how often she encountered those places.
"Often enough," she said. "But I stopped logging them after a while. You put that kind of thing in a report, it doesn't go anywhere good."

In 1986, a Parks Canada motion camera placed near the Flat River bend recorded a 36-hour period where **no motion was captured** — not even wind-blown grass. The batteries were fine. Weather logs show no storms. When they retrieved the camera, the SD card was intact, but the timecode had looped. It showed "00:00:00" for 17 hours. Then it resumed normally. No tampering. No damage. Just missing time.

Predators seem to follow invisible fences. Wolves skirt certain ridgelines. Moose tracks stop clean at the edge of burn circles. Bears — usually fearless and territorial — turn back from specific river branches with no sign of threat.

One field note, from a 2007 Yukon biologist:
"Observed black bear abruptly halt movement at 0933. Raised head. Turned 180 degrees. Did not return to area. Checked site. No immediate environmental cue present. Recorded EMF anomaly on handheld scanner. Battery dropped from 100% to 12%."

I found four more examples. Different species. Different years. Same result. Animals *choose* not to go. And animals don't rationalize fear. They obey something deeper.

The Dene elders I spoke to refused to hunt in certain places — even when the game signs were strong just outside them. One told me,
"The deer don't go there because they still remember what we've forgotten."
She didn't elaborate.

Some places are unsafe. Others are *uninviting*. Nahanni has zones that push even the wild away.

And if the animals aren't going there, neither should we.

But I am.

And I'm bringing a camera.

Chapter 7 – The Uncounted

There are names that never made the list. No case numbers. No press releases. Just absence.

In every major wilderness with a history of disappearances, there's a pattern: some names go missing from the world — others go missing from the record. The Nahanni has both.

I found the first during a deep scan of 1950s-era outfitter logs — back when records were handwritten, sometimes just notes on the backs of fuel manifests. There was a name: **Lyle Mathers**, scrawled next to a red check mark and the words *"did not return — no next of kin."* No official follow-up. No missing-person report in the archives. Just that one quiet mark, like an afterthought. Lyle Mathers never existed anywhere else. No census. No family search hits. One line. Then nothing.

The second came from a trapper's journal, left behind in an abandoned shack south of the Ram Plateau. In it, he lists supply drops from the late '60s. Most are mundane: flour, salt, ammo, tobacco. But every entry ends with a name. One name appears five times: **"Jonas."** No last name. Then, on the sixth entry, it just says:
"Jonas didn't show. Left the tin anyway. Cold as hell."
That was January 1972. The next entry is written in a different hand, with a shaking pen:
"Don't leave tins for ghosts."

That trapper was never identified. The shack was destroyed in a controlled burn in the 1990s. The journal was rescued by a climber and passed anonymously into a regional folklore archive.

These people — Lyle, Jonas, and others like them — don't show up in the usual places. They're **unofficial disappearances**. But they ripple. They leave **echoes** in field logs, trail reports, radio snippets, and rumors passed around campfires and ranger stations. They're the ones rangers remember late at night but won't write down.

In 2011, a SAR volunteer I spoke with mentioned a man who vanished without ever being reported missing.
"He was the kind of guy who wouldn't check in," the volunteer said. "But he always checked out. Until that trip."
No formal search. No closure. Just a friend waiting too long, then packing up his tent and driving home.

I ran what I had through the AI. Gave it scattered fragments — date ranges, locations, references in journals, local oral accounts. I didn't expect much. But it built a heat map. A cluster of disappearances that *weren't in any official registry*. It flagged them as "likely factual but unrecorded." That was the phrase: **"Likely factual."**

I asked it why the disappearances went uncounted.
The model returned one line:
"Source ecosystem may not support persistent external memory."

I stared at that sentence for a long time.

In most places, memory is recorded by humans.

In Nahanni, it seems to be recorded by **something else** — and it decides what stays forgotten.

Chapter 8 – Things Found That Shouldn't Be

Disappearance is one kind of mystery. Discovery is another.

Every wilderness has its lost things: tools dropped in rivers, gloves left behind, tents torn by weather. That's normal. But in Nahanni, the problem isn't what gets left behind — it's **what gets returned**. Or worse… **what turns up without a story.**

Take the 1965 gold pan found 20 kilometers off any known trail. Clean. Unused. No oxidization. Stamped "D. Mcleod" — a name linked to a prospector who vanished in 1908. The RCMP dismissed it as forgery. A historian I spoke to said the stamping tool used hadn't existed until 1919. And yet, the pan was real. It sat in a university archive for years before being quietly lost. The shelf log now simply reads: *"Relocated."*

Then there's the camera. Found in 1992 by a hiking group near the Stone Knife River. Nikon F2. Broken shutter. No strap. But the film inside was intact. The images were developed in Yellowknife: ten photos. The last five completely black. The first five showed a forested path… and then one image with a man standing in frame. His back turned. Shirtless. Skin pale. Hands at his side. Blurred — as if vibrating. No one recognized him. The timestamp read 1976.

The most disturbing part? The model of film inside the camera was discontinued in 1983.

In 2007, a survey team found a compass. Still pointing — but the needle was spinning slowly, clockwise. A loop every twenty-eight seconds. The case was worn. The initials "K.B." scratched into the back. No one on the team matched the initials. They turned it in. It vanished from the station inventory two weeks later.

There's also the matter of the shoes. Found at the base of a granite outcrop in 2015 by a geology student. Weathered hiking boots, laces perfectly tied. No wear on the soles. Clean — almost suspiciously so. One was half-filled with river pebbles. The other had a folded piece of paper inside. No writing. Just folded. When tested, the paper was found to be 100% pure cellulose — no ink, no water damage, no origin tag. As if it had never been made.

Even more disturbing than these objects are the ones returned **to people**.

A solo hiker named Adrian Case lost his GPS unit during a river crossing. Gone under. Submerged. Gone. Four days later, he found it — sitting upright outside his tent. Dry. Screen flashing a blank coordinate:
"00.0000°N 00.0000°E."
He left the valley the next day.

I compiled these objects. Tracked them. Tried to locate them. Most are gone. Taken into archives. Lost in university storage. Some were "misfiled." Others never existed according to their last handlers. My AI flagged them as **"non-attributable anomalies."** One note in the diagnostic summary stood out:

"Presence of artifacts inconsistent with known human logistical routes."

Things found in places that no one could reach.

Things with no trace of who brought them… or who came to take them back.

Nahanni doesn't just swallow. Sometimes it **spits back.**

And when it does — it chooses what to reveal.

Chapter 9 – The River Remembers

If the valley is the body, the river is its spine.

The South Nahanni River is 563 kilometers of cold, muscular water — winding through limestone gorges, carving between mountains, and surging past landmarks with names that sound more like warnings than tourist stops. Deadmen Valley. Funeral Range. Headless Creek.

This isn't a lazy backcountry stream. It's a moving archive.

Every mystery in Nahanni eventually finds its way to water.

Bodies, when they surface, don't follow the laws of current. The McLeod brothers were found *upriver* from their last known location. In 1945, a canoe was found washed up with food still sealed and dry in its watertight barrel — but no sign of its paddler, whose body was recovered weeks later *inland*, miles from any navigable branch. In 1983, a SAR diver working near Virginia Falls reported feeling "something pulling downward" in an eddy pool no deeper than five meters. His partner thought it was panic. The diver still swears something moved below him — *with intent*.

Locals talk about the river as if it's alive. Not metaphorically — literally. One elder told me, *"That water can hear. And it doesn't forget."*
I asked him if he meant the land holds memory.
"No," he said. "The land forgets. The river keeps it. Just doesn't share."

Geologically, the Nahanni is ancient. Pre-glacial. It carved its path before the last Ice Age and then kept it. But something about that path resists mapping. Canoeists log GPS drifts of up to 300 meters. In one case, two kayakers tried to replicate a previous route using exact coordinates. The second team couldn't find two of the rapids. They had been swallowed. The terrain was the same. The water, somehow… wasn't.

I interviewed a hydrologist who had taken samples during a Parks Canada study. She noticed temperature fluctuations that didn't match any seasonal model. Cold pockets moved like living things — warm upflows vanished mid-scan. "It felt like it didn't want to be measured," she told me. "Like it knew."

That word again: *intent*.

The river is always moving — but what it chooses to carry, and what it gives back, doesn't follow the logic of nature. It follows a different rhythm. A deeper one.

I once watched a log float by that had no bark and no moss, but grooves on its side — like hands had gripped it, then let go. I didn't record it. I didn't need to.

Because that's the thing.

The river remembers for you.

And sometimes, it remembers what shouldn't be remembered.

Chapter 10 – Witnesses Who Lied

Not everyone who came back told the truth.

When you research disappearances, one of the hardest things isn't proving who's missing — it's making sense of who's left behind. The ones who claim to know what happened. The ones who swear they saw nothing. The ones who change their story, once, twice, sometimes three times.

Some are just scared. That's forgivable. But others lie with intent.

Take the 1951 survey incident. Two junior geologists were mapping glacial erosion sites near First Canyon. Only one returned. The survivor, Thomas Ward, said his partner slipped during a climb. Died instantly. The body was "unrecoverable." No SAR team was ever launched. The case was shelved as an accident.

Fifty years later, Ward's nephew donated a box of old notebooks to a university archive. One journal had a scratched-out passage that, when lifted with digital filters, read:
"He was looking into the rocks. Said they were hollow. Said he saw someone moving. I told him to stop. He didn't."

That was the last entry. Dated two days after the reported "fall."

Ward's accident report never mentioned rocks. Or movement. Just a slip.

Another case: 1979, American hiker named Hal Simms. Claimed he soloed into Deadmen Valley and spent five nights alone. His photos were off — timestamped with dates from two months prior. When pressed, he admitted he'd doctored them. Said he'd "lost" the original film. Later confessed he never reached the valley floor. "I couldn't go through with it," he told a local guide. "Felt like I was being watched from under the dirt."

Why lie? Why come back and make up a story when the truth is already strange enough?

Because sometimes, I think, the lies are safer. They're a way to put a wall between the witness and whatever they actually saw.

One ranger, retired now, told me about a group of four who camped just south of The Curve in the mid-90s. Only three returned. Their official statement said the fourth turned back early. But their outfitter noted he'd flown all four of them *in*. And *no one* flew back out early. The RCMP report ended with the word: **"Discrepancy noted."**

When I tried to contact the group — two were dead. One refused to speak. Said, *"It didn't happen like they said. But I'll never say what did."*

Even my AI model struggled with these cases. Testimonies flagged as **"conflictive narrative fragments."** In other words: the facts don't agree with each other. Or with reality. And not just small mistakes. *Big ones*. Like weather conditions that didn't match records. Moon phases off by two nights. People remembering landscapes that don't exist on any map.

One case involved a prospector who swore he saw "an entire cabin blink out." His partner said no such structure existed. They drew maps of the same route. They didn't match.

Someone was lying. Or both were telling the truth… about different versions of the same place.

I used to think lies were the problem.

Now I wonder if they're the only way people can describe the impossible — without breaking themselves.

Chapter 11 – Fire Doesn't Behave Here

In the wilderness, fire is everything. It's warmth. Safety. Signal. Control. It's the oldest form of human power.

In Nahanni, fire becomes something else.

Accounts go back as far as the early trappers. Journal entries mention "flickering flames that won't hold," or matches that burn but refuse to ignite tinder. Even modern camp stoves sputter and misfire for no reason — only to work again miles away. One search and rescue team logged a strange flare event in 2003 where a magnesium torch ignited, *but made no light*. It burned. It hissed. But the darkness remained.

I've experienced this myself.

Night three, upstream of Glacier Lake. The lighter caught. The flame held. But the firewood wouldn't take — not even birch bark soaked in fuel gel. It just smoldered, slowly… like it was being watched. Then I heard a pop — soft, like a knuckle cracking — and suddenly the whole pile went up at once, all at the wrong angles. Sideways flames. Heat but no smoke. The air smelled *metallic*.

I didn't sleep that night.

In 1982, a fire tower operator reported a "moving burn." A slow, circular ignition that traveled *against* wind direction and uphill. The fire line would vanish, then reappear behind itself. He logged it as a probable heat mirage. But when he went down to inspect the area, the soil was scorched in a perfect ring. Ten feet across. Nothing in the center was touched.

The Dene talk about "ghost fires." Not metaphor. Actual phenomenon. Flames that rise in places where no fuel exists. They aren't feared — but they are avoided. One elder told me, *"Those fires remember. And sometimes they look back."*

In 1999, a pilot flying out of Tungsten at dusk saw what he believed to be a flare. He turned to investigate, fearing a stranded hiker. The light vanished. Later review of flight path GPS logs showed the object was *above* the tree line — at roughly 400 feet elevation. No source. No smoke. Just heat and red flash.

The AI found sixteen separate reports of anomalous flame patterns between 1947 and 2018. Most near canyon walls or along specific bends in the river. Common tags: *"inverted burn direction," "sound delay during ignition," "light without heat,"* and in three cases: *"flame movement independent of wind."*

In one archived SAR report, a team member describes a campsite that was "burned from the inside out." The fire ring was intact. The grass outside the ring untouched. But the **center of the ring** was charred deep into the soil — almost to ash.

This isn't just strange fire behavior.

This is fire with intention.

Fire that answers to **different physics**.

Or worse — fire that's remembering a **different set of rules.**

Chapter 12 – The Ridge No One Climbs

They don't give it a name on maps.

Not an official one, anyway. To geologists, it's just another spine of Devonian limestone running east of the Vampire Peaks. Coordinates place it neatly — elevation gradient, average slope, rock type. All standard.

But in field journals, travel logs, and verbal warnings passed between river guides, it has a different identity: **The Ridge No One Climbs.**

It isn't the tallest. It isn't the steepest. And it doesn't appear any more dangerous than its neighbors. But the stories around it echo with one shared rule: *"Don't go up."*

The first record I found was in a disintegrating 1959 trapper's map — the kind with hand-drawn X's and coffee stains. One peak was simply marked with a red line and the word: *"bad."*

I dismissed it — until I found a 1973 DND flight log describing "aerospace interference" during a training flyover. The plane's sensors scrambled just over that ridge. HUD reset. Altimeter froze. The onboard camera recorded one second of visual static. Then everything returned to normal. No mechanical damage. But the pilot refused to fly that route again.

A former outfitter told me flat out: "Nobody summits it. Not in the thirty years I worked the valley. Not once." I asked why. He shrugged. "Things stop working up there. Minds, mostly."

One hiker in 2005 tried to climb it alone. His partner stayed behind. The plan was simple: ascend, mark elevation, return. It was a clear day. He carried a radio, GPS, and two compasses.

He never came back.

Searchers found his camp. Found a boot track leading toward the ridge's western rise. Then it stopped. Not disappeared — *stopped*. Like the person who made it had lifted off the earth.

No gear was ever recovered.

More than one rescue report notes weather shifts around the ridge. High-pressure distortion. Fog that doesn't move. Cold air that falls in vertical columns like water.

The AI flagged this zone when I inputted unmarked incident coordinates. It returned a heat map — cold in the center. Like a hole in the data. Not empty. *Absorbing*.

When I ran that same input with satellite overlays, the terrain glitched. Once. A horizontal strip of static. It corrected itself in three seconds. But I recorded the clip. Something there doesn't want to be seen from above.

And maybe that's the rule.

The Ridge doesn't take lives the way rivers or storms do. It takes curiosity. Ambition. It waits.

Because something doesn't want to be reached.

And something up there… climbs **back**.

Chapter 13 – The Creek That Changed Direction

There is a creek that appears on all historic maps of the Nahanni Valley, flowing southward toward the main artery of the river system. Shallow, slow-moving, and largely unremarkable, it has been marked for over a century in both handwritten journals and modern topographic data. Surveyors noted it in 1907. Bush pilots used it as a visual marker. Even recent satellite imagery confirms its gentle southern flow.

And yet in 1996, a geological reconnaissance team noted something strange. The creek was flowing north.

There had been no recent landslides. No seismic activity. The surrounding terrain showed no uplift or rerouting. The elevation remained consistent. And yet the current moved uphill—against the established slope and away from the river basin it had always fed.

Photographs taken that summer show leaves drifting slowly northward. Flow markers confirmed directional reversal. Field notes logged confusion, but no conclusions. The anomaly lasted three days. Then the water stopped.

When the team returned two weeks later, the creek bed was dry. The surrounding ground showed no evidence of drainage or evaporation. What had once been a navigational reference point had simply ceased to exist. No water. No movement. Nothing.

Where the water once passed, they found a cairn of five stones stacked deliberately at the bend. Beneath them, a rusted compass retrieved from a previous expedition—its needle no longer fixed to magnetic north, but circling, slowly, in silence.

Locals who heard the story called it "the wandering flow," and mentioned that such reversals had happened before—but only during certain times. Times when the wind over the valley paused for too long. Or when the river below turned quiet enough to hear something else.

Something inside the ground.

Chapter 14 – The Room with No Walls

Fred Bower said it first.

After three weeks of silence in a hospital bed, he looked up at the ceiling and whispered, *"It showed me a room with no walls."*

I wrote that down when I first read his notes. It felt cryptic. Metaphorical. Maybe the rambling of a traumatized mind. But lately, I've started seeing that phrase show up in other places — scrawled in field notebooks, whispered in fragments during interviews, even suggested in AI anomaly tags: *"spatial disassociation event."*

I didn't understand it.

Until I stood in one.

Not literally. Not physically. But something happened upstream from Glacier Lake. Just before dawn. I was alone, walking the treeline to clear my head before packing camp. There was no fog. No wind. The air was so still it felt artificial.

Then… something folded.

I don't know how else to describe it. The treeline around me didn't move. The sky didn't change. But the **space** did. A pressure, like the inside of a bell jar. My ears popped — not from elevation, but silence. I couldn't hear birds. Or my own boots. Or even my breath. The world didn't go quiet. It went *removed*.

And that's when it hit me: I wasn't in danger. I wasn't lost.

I was being **held.**

It lasted maybe ten seconds. Or ten minutes. It's hard to say. Time in that moment didn't behave. When it ended, I stumbled forward — back into sound, into the real world — and nearly vomited. The treeline was the same. My pack untouched. No signs of movement.

But every photo I took that morning came out blurred — **except one**.

It shows an empty clearing, a low haze of blue light, and a smudge that can't be explained by motion blur or lens error. It's centered. Geometric. Like a doorway made of heat.

I haven't shown it to anyone.

I don't know what it means. But I know this: the Room with No Walls isn't a hallucination. It's not poetic metaphor. It's a real place — or maybe a condition — that some part of Nahanni can invoke.

Bower wasn't mad.

He was the first to name it.

And I think it's waiting for me to return.

Chapter 15 – Patterns in the Bone Dust

Bones tell stories long after the voice is gone.

Most wilderness deaths are blunt and final. Missteps. Exposure. Falls. Animals. When searchers find remains, the patterns are usually obvious — trauma signatures, animal tooth marks, time-of-death decay.

But in Nahanni, some of the remains that have turned up don't fit any of that.

In 1971, a skull was found just outside Rabbitkettle Lake. No mandible. No connective tissue. No signs of animal predation. Clean — but not polished by weather. Just *absent*. The pathologist wrote: *"unusual lack of connective residue."* No ID was ever confirmed.

In 1998, a partial femur and tibia were found near Deadmen Valley — separated by thirty feet. Both bones were snapped clean, like from a fall. But there were no cliffs nearby. The surrounding area was flat. And the breaks showed no signs of bone bruising — meaning the fractures occurred **post-mortem**, under low-pressure force. One forensics expert I interviewed called it "surgical but impossible."

Then there was the hiker in 2006. They found only vertebrae and a boot. Inside the boot, packed neatly, were river stones. The coroner's report used a phrase I hadn't seen before: *"Remains exhibit non-random scatter consistent with intentional placement."*

That phrase stopped me.

Because if the scatter is **intentional**, then the agent is intelligent. And if it's intelligent, it's either human… or something acting with purpose.

The AI flagged this category as "anomalous ossuary events." It compared bone dispersion ratios from wilderness remains across North America and found a **statistically improbable cluster** in Nahanni — particularly near blind canyons and river junctions.

I overlaid this data with known Dene oral traditions.

One phrase came up again and again: *"Where the bones look back."*

There are accounts of burial sites that move. Ossuaries that vanish. A ranger once told me about finding a ribcage splayed out on a rock — no skull, no legs — and when he returned to mark it, it was gone. The rock was clean. But when he photographed it later that night with a night-vision trail cam, something showed up: a soft white outline, like dust caught in an eddy. A pattern. Almost floral.

Bone dust doesn't just scatter. Sometimes, it **forms**.

I believe some of what's been left behind in Nahanni isn't the result of death — but of **removal**. A ritual we don't understand. Or a process we were never meant to witness.

It's not that these people weren't found.

It's that they were **presented.**

And whatever did it didn't care if we understood.

Only that we looked.

Chapter 16 – The Ice Doesn't Keep Them

Cold is supposed to preserve.

In the north, the rule is simple: if something dies in the cold, it stays. Bodies freeze, decay halts, and searchers know they'll find what they're looking for — even if it takes a season. The ice keeps things. Even in death, there's **stillness**.

But in Nahanni, that stillness doesn't hold.

In 1963, a floatplane pilot spotted a downed tent in a basin between two minor peaks near Glacier Lake. Inside were two sleeping bags. Only one was occupied. The man was dead — hands still gripping the sleeping bag zipper, face frozen in panic. But the forensic team found something strange: his skin temperature was *far above* what it should've been after three days exposed to -12°C. No signs of fire. No residual body heat. Internal organs intact. Just **warm skin.** As if something had delayed the cold — or replaced it.

In 1987, a snowshoe guide vanished on a solo circuit near the Flat River fork. He wore a beacon, but it never activated. Eight months later, a Dene family found his body intact in a melt pool — no bloating, no breakdown. Clothing dry. But the beacon was *gone*. The pouch had been cut open with surgical precision. Not torn. Not damaged. Removed.

Then came 2009.

That was the body pulled from the edge of a thawed permafrost slab — discolored, wet, and unidentifiable. But not from rot. From *alteration*. The teeth were missing, but not broken. Extracted. Every fingernail was filed flat. No bruising. The hair was gone. Not shaven — removed at the follicle. Like something had **harvested** parts of the man and gently laid him back. The autopsy report was redacted. All that remained in the release was one phrase:
"No signs of frostbite."

That phrase haunts me.

The AI helped me analyze glacial thaw trends in Nahanni. It flagged temperature anomalies in melt rate — but only near known disappearance zones. Ice that should last decades vanishing in seasons. And in some cases, reverse: shallow ice holding for years despite ambient warming.

One hydrologist said it best: *"It's like something's tampering with time. Or with the cold itself."*

I interviewed an elder who once watched a body emerge from a spring thaw — only to see it vanish again a week later.

"It doesn't like to keep things where we can find them," she said. *"It wants them soft, not stiff."*

There's something about the ice in Nahanni.

It doesn't preserve. It recycles.

Chapter 17 – They Carried Something Back

Not everyone who goes missing in Nahanni stays missing.

Some return.

They walk out of the bush under their own power. Sometimes days after a planned exit. Sometimes weeks. Once, twenty-seven days past expected return, without food or frostbite. They're always found close to trailheads or rivers — never deep inside. But their stories don't add up.

In 1977, a hunter named Marcel Fontaine disappeared during a solo moose expedition. Heavy snow. No beacon. The search was called off after nine days. On the twelfth day, he was found walking calmly beside a mining road. Coat unzipped. No frostbite. He didn't speak for three days. When he finally did, he said, *"I heard my own name from beneath the ice. It told me where to walk."*

In 1992, a woman named C. B. (her initials are all I was given) went into Nahanni with a church group. She broke away from the main trail. Vanished. Forty-eight hours later, she was spotted by helicopter — standing in a shallow bend of the river. Arms stiff at her side. Eyes closed. When they landed, she didn't respond to her name. When they carried her out, she whispered just one thing: *"It wasn't a dream. It was older than that."*

She never returned to the North.

Then came the SAR volunteer in 2010. He fell through a snowbank during a recovery op and vanished from sight. Rope line pulled slack. He was found ninety minutes later — upright, twenty feet uphill from where he disappeared. His boots were on the wrong feet. His radio was tuned to a frequency never used in the field: 173.700 MHz. No one could explain how it happened. He retired two weeks later and refused interviews.

Some return different.

Personality changes. No eye contact. Light sensitivity. Repetitive speech. One man drew a spiral on his arm every morning for three months. Another stopped sleeping indoors. He said the **walls got too close.**

I fed forty-six survivor reports into the AI — cross-analyzing medical, psychological, and testimonial data. It flagged seventeen of them with a shared behavioral tag:
"Semantic dislocation: high."

That means the words they use don't match normal trauma profiles. It's not PTSD. It's **rewiring**.

One quote stood out. A woman from Whitehorse, recovered in 2001 after six days missing. Her hands were covered in black dust. She said, *"I didn't find something. Something found me. And then it told me to forget."*

But she hadn't. She'd just stopped **telling**.

I believe some of these people brought something back — not physical, but informational. Like a pattern. A frequency. A suggestion buried in the folds of thought.

Not a possession.

A **download**.

And I think I've started to feel it too.

Chapter 18 – The Ones Who Stayed

Some vanish.
Some crawl back out.
But a few — a very specific few — **stay**.

They aren't listed as missing. Not in any official registry. Their permits expire. Their mail stops forwarding. But there's no SAR alert. No grieving families. Just a quiet blank where a person used to be.

I call them the **silent stay-behinds**.

In 1974, a seasonal geologist named Ernest Deroux wintered alone in a log cabin south of Ram Creek. He radioed in weekly, always punctual, until the spring melt. Then silence. A helicopter team found the cabin fully stocked. Stove cold. Bed made. No sign of departure. But on the kitchen table was a single note:
"Still warm. Staying longer."

He was never seen again.

In 1985, a hiker known only as "Marcus" came in with a permit under a fake name. The ranger noted he asked unusually specific questions about moon cycles and river echoes. Three weeks later, his gear was found lashed to a tree with ceremonial knots — Dene in origin, but arranged **incorrectly**, like someone was copying a pattern they didn't fully understand. A short entry was found in his notebook:
"I finally see the shape. It's everywhere."

1996: A canoe was found moored with surgical precision near a hard-to-reach bend east of The Curve. Inside were dry bags of untouched food, medical supplies, and a satellite radio with the antenna removed. Tied to the seat with paracord was a paperback book: *The Mothman Prophecies*, opened to a page about "window areas." Written in the margin was one line:
"If I leave, it forgets me. If I stay, it teaches."

There's no evidence these people died. But there's no evidence they *left*, either.

I asked the AI to scan field reports and ranger interviews for the term "voluntary no-return." It returned 23 entries with qualifying flags — all clustered within five decades. Most around The Curve, Deadmen Valley, and the "ridge with no name."

What separates them from the missing is intent.

You don't stay in Nahanni by accident.
Not without food. Not without contact. Not without being changed.

Some of them **wanted** to vanish.
Others were given **a reason to remain**.

One ex-guide, now a recluse, once told me in a moment of unfiltered honesty:
"Some don't leave because they weren't meant to. Something in there… sees them. Picks them. And they feel that recognition. For the first time in their lives."

I asked if that had happened to him.

He didn't answer.

But when I left, he whispered:
"It only teaches the ones who don't tell."

Chapter 19 – If You Hear Your Name

It's almost always the same.

A lone hiker. A field worker. Sometimes a trained SAR volunteer. Someone out past twilight, pausing beside the river or halfway into the treeline. And then…

They hear it.

Their name.

Not shouted. Not whispered. **Spoken.**

And always from the wrong direction.

Every region has its share of unsettling folklore, but in Nahanni this particular story doesn't stay in the realm of myth. It repeats. Quietly. Across decades. Across disciplines. Some have told no one. Others leave mid-expedition without explanation. One guide described it as *"a voice that skips the ears and lands behind your eyes."*

I encountered this pattern by accident.

Inputting text logs into the AI, I noticed a cluster of field journals with phrases like *"Heard name – no source,"* or *"Felt spoken to – not local,"* or, in three separate documents across thirty years: *"Sounded like my mother."*

When the system filtered for phrase recurrence, one line stood out:

"It called me by my full name."

That phrase appears in testimonies going back to 1940. Different sources. Different languages. Different professions.

Always the same feeling:

- A sudden stillness
- No animals
- A directional confusion
- And then the voice

- Familiar, but not correct

One man said it sounded like his brother… but hollow. Another said it was *her own voice*, but slower. And a third, a fire technician, refused to describe it, only writing:
"I heard it. I know what it wants. I won't answer again."

I asked one elder from Fort Liard if she'd ever heard of the voice.

She said, simply:
"If you hear your name, walk faster."

There are no known deaths linked directly to the voice. But there are dozens of **directional disorientation cases** that begin shortly after the event. In some cases, GPS data shows the person veering away from known trails — not in panic, but in slow, consistent arcs. As if **being led**.

I believe the voice is not a hallucination.

It's a kind of bait. A signal. Something that reaches into memory and *pulls the one name that matters most*. Yours.

And it's never loud.

It's just close.

Chapter 20 – The Last Map Doesn't Match

The first inconsistencies appeared in the cartographic archives — old Parks Canada maps, regional topographic surveys, and geological data layered across decades.

In a 1972 elevation chart, a ridge near the Flat River is clearly marked. It appears again in a 1986 hiking atlas, noted for its use as a windbreak. By 2004, the ridge is gone. Not worn down. Not eroded. Simply **absent** from the data.

It doesn't stop there.

One floodplain near The Curve is listed as "unstable terrain" on the 1991 SAR overlay. But a 2013 mining survey labels it "solid rock basin." The coordinates are identical. The landscape is not.

Across five decades, dozens of such mismatches appear — bends in rivers that no longer exist, tributaries that diverge without topographic reason, even altitude readings that fluctuate without tectonic justification. An especially troubling case involves a 1997 fire crew who recorded a glacial ridge for aerial mapping. The recorded footage shows a wide clearing with a horseshoe lake.

Today, the same coordinates display only **dense forest**. No ridge. No lake. No clearing.

The AI ran a composite overlay using 15 data sources — from DND flight logs to hydrological maps — and flagged 19 distinct "cartographic conflict zones." Six of these conflict zones align with long-term disappearances. Three correspond to known rescue locations. And two have no known event on record… only **silence**.

In 2009, a GPS-guided camera retrieved from a deceased hiker recorded dozens of images from a valley bend that **doesn't exist**. The metadata was clean. The signal solid. Yet the imagery shows a terrain type never mapped in that region — jagged slate walls, a reflective water body, and what appears to be the shape of a rock shelter. Geologists could not identify the formation. None have found it since.

Field reports describe hikers walking due west and ending north. Compasses that spin. Stars that refuse to line up with location. And, in rare cases, **people describing terrain features that predate known glacial shifts.**

One backcountry outfitter refused to speak on record but offered this:
"It's not that the land moves. It's that you're not always invited to see it the same way twice."

A former survey pilot who flew the region from 1988 to 2010 reported HUD distortions and altimeter errors when crossing certain unnamed ridgelines. In one case, a deep canyon appeared on radar where there was none. He descended to confirm — and found only mist and empty forest.

Perhaps the most mysterious record comes from a 2004 fire survey. It includes a hand-annotated canyon labeled "Void Corridor." The canyon appears only on that single map. There is no trace of it in modern terrain data. The surrounding area is flat.

Attempts to confirm the canyon's existence have failed.

It seems even the **land** in Nahanni knows how to forget.

Chapter 21 – Shadow at Noon

In most of the northern wilderness, the sun tells the truth. It rises, it arcs, it sets. Shadows stretch predictably. Orientation is easy. You can trust the light.

But in Nahanni, light doesn't always follow the rules.

Reports of "wrong shadows" date back nearly a century. In 1929, a Dominion land surveyor sketched an incident in his notebook: *"Sun high above, but shadow cast west. No obstruction. Shadow unmoving for five minutes."* The entry ends abruptly. The next page begins a full three days later.

A guide in 1970 noted that while preparing lunch on a clear, windless day, a shadow moved across his cooking pot *"as if someone had walked behind him."* He turned. Nothing. Then he noticed: the shadow wasn't his. It was longer. It moved **against** the sun.

He left the valley that week and never returned.

The phenomenon is not limited to direct sunlight. In 2001, a wildlife tech using thermal imaging spotted what appeared to be **a heat void** — not a body, not an animal — just **an absence**, shaped like a man, standing upright. It cast a shadow across moss, yet the infrared showed no heat signature. And when she blinked, it was gone.

In another case, a fire crew in 2013 was forced to halt operations after multiple team members reported "overlapping shadows" during peak daylight — shadows that crisscrossed without movement. Their logs recorded it as *"optical fatigue."*

But the AI saw more.

When prompted with terms like *"false shadow,"* *"displaced silhouette,"* and *"inverted sun position,"* it clustered 14 incidents from 1956–2020 within a 60km corridor along the Flat River. All occurred within ±30 minutes of solar noon. That detail — **timing** — repeats across unconnected testimonies. The moment when light should be at its most stable is when the distortions begin.

A particularly unsettling case occurred in 1998, when a geologist reported seeing his own shadow duplicate — splitting slightly off to the side, then snapping back. He wrote:
"It was me, but more tired. Like it had been walking longer."

An elder from the Nahanni Butte area described it more simply:
"Sometimes the sun looks down and something looks back up."

There are no photographs of these shadows. Not reliable ones. Cameras fail. Exposures blur. But the stories persist. Some say they saw multiple shadows belonging to a single person. Others saw none at all. A few heard footsteps that matched the length of their shadow — as if it was pacing them.

Whatever causes it, one thing is certain:

In Nahanni, the sun doesn't always shine **alone**.

And when shadows appear at noon…
it means something else is **standing in your light.**

Chapter 22 – The Sound the Ground Makes

It doesn't shake trees.
It doesn't register on seismic sensors.
And yet — the ground in Nahanni sometimes **speaks**.

Not with words. Not even with audible sound, always. But with something deeper. Something **felt** in the bones before it ever touches the ears. A pressure. A vibration. A low, alien pulse beneath the moss and stone.

The first account on record dates to 1938, found in a faded trapper's journal:
"Heard the land grumble. Not thunder. Not mine work. The earth breathed once — deep — then went still."

Since then, the accounts have only grown stranger.

In 1967, two fire surveyors near Glacier Lake reported a sensation like a slow roll beneath their feet. The air was dead calm. Trees didn't sway. And yet, one of them vomited. The other claimed to feel his **heartbeat change tempo**, syncing with something low and rhythmic. They radioed in for evac, but by the time the chopper arrived, the sensation had stopped.

Their soil samples later showed no tectonic disturbance.

In 1994, a research tent collapsed during a night of still weather. Not from wind — the stakes had **risen** out of the ground. The team lead said the soil "fluttered," like the surface of a drumskin. One technician compared it to "a subwoofer buried under the tundra."

When the reports were digitized and fed into the anomaly model, a pattern emerged.

The sounds — when mapped — cluster around **three known disappearance zones** and **two semi-permanent glacial fissures**. They occur not during storms, but during periods of **unbroken atmospheric silence**. The AI flagged the events under a unique internal tag:
"Non-seismic subsonic terrain pulse."

And then there are the phrases survivors use.

- "Like a big cat purring under gravel."

- "Felt like something woke up beneath me."

- "It buzzed in my feet. Not my ears."

- "The ground was... listening."

One SAR team member, during a 2007 missing person case, described the forest as *"dead silent except for the ground itself."*
He later added, *"I think we walked on something we weren't supposed to."*

Indigenous knowledge systems from the area don't contradict these events — they *predict* them. Dene elders speak of places where the land "dreams inward," where animals refuse to tread, and where "the earth remembers things it hasn't shown yet."

Not echoes.

Memory.

And that might be the most unsettling part.

This isn't sound as we understand it. It's a kind of **intelligence transmission** through vibration — a territorial heartbeat. It isn't warning or greeting.

It's presence.

And sometimes, if you're still enough...
you feel it listening back.

Chapter 23 – The Ones Who Drew Maps Too Late

There's a drawer at the Glenbow Archives in Calgary labeled:
"Unfinished Cartography – Northwest District, 1902–1974."

Inside are fragile maps — some penciled on surveyor vellum, others scratched into leather, one traced into birch bark. Nearly all contain markings related to Nahanni. And none of them are finished.

A 1911 exploration party led by Cpl. Frederick Maguire set out with full surveying instruments, government sponsorship, and a mandate to "rectify anomalies in Dominion topography." Only three men returned. Their maps were stained, fragmented. Rivers curved where they shouldn't. Peaks shifted mid-sketch. One included a note scribbled near Deadmen Valley:
"Chart halts here. Too much movement."

In 1935, an Austrian-born cartographer named Wilhelm Grube spent four months sketching a topographical mural of the southern Nahanni range. It was supposed to hang in the federal museum. What arrived instead was a chaotic wash of lines, overlapping ridges, and an unnerving set of repeating shapes in the margins — **concentric eyes**.

Grube was later hospitalized. He claimed the land had changed **while he was drawing it**.

Decades later, in 1969, a military mapping aircraft from CFB Cold Lake conducted a high-resolution aerial survey over Nahanni. Midway through the flight, the camera system malfunctioned. Every exposure taken above a specific valley came back **black** — not blank, not overexposed — pitch black. As if nothing had reflected.

The official report concluded "optical malfunction due to high-angle sunlight." But two of the technicians involved never flew again. One later described the area as "a place that erases you from altitude."

Field sketchbooks from amateur geologists show similar stories: rivers that shift positions between days, tree lines that grow **too fast**, and outcroppings that vanish by the time the ink dries.

The AI compared incomplete maps to modern LIDAR scans. It found discrepancies not just in elevation, but in **contour logic** — the angle and rise of land where none should exist. In some scans, a ridge curves subtly inward, forming a shape not consistent with erosion… but with **architecture**.

No one's ever confirmed it.

Perhaps most unsettling is a 1983 sketch recovered from a missing anthropologist's belongings — mailed posthumously from Fort Nelson. It contains no topographic data. Just a circle of symbols, labeled in small script:
"The map that draws itself when you aren't looking."

He was never found.

These were people trained to measure, define, and commit the wild to paper.

But Nahanni doesn't want to be drawn.

And it seems to know when it's being watched.

Chapter 24 – The Disappearances That Rewrote the Timeline

Some vanishings in Nahanni are tragic.
Some are inexplicable.
But a rare few are something else entirely:

Unclassifiable.
Events that break sequence. Appear before their cause. Leave behind details that shouldn't exist — or shouldn't exist *yet*.

These are the cases that **bend time**.

In 1953, a prospector named Ivan Leduc was reported missing after radio silence near the western slope of Deadmen Valley. A search party found no trace. The case went cold. But in 1957 — four years later — a park ranger found Leduc's hat and pickaxe resting against a stone cairn. Both were clean. Unweathered. Inside the hat was a Polaroid photo… of a logging site that wouldn't be built until 1959.

No camera was ever recovered.

In 1971, a botanist vanished 16 kilometers into the Grotto Basin. Her journal, found months later, included a detailed drawing of a plant species no one could identify. She called it *"Silvervine."* It wasn't until 2002 that researchers discovered a mutation in alpine fireweed matching the drawing exactly — triggered by warming patterns that **didn't exist in the '70s.**

In 1990, three hikers disappeared after splitting off from their group near the Glacier Fork. No distress call. No bad weather. Just silence. Fifteen days later, one of their sleeping bags was found folded neatly under a rock overhang. Inside was a ranger field guide from **2014** — twenty-four years in the future. The printing data was verified. The publisher swore the guide hadn't been designed yet. It was an exact match.

There was no explanation. The bag was placed into evidence and later misplaced. Official logs state only:
"Unusual paper stock. Suspected forgery. No follow-up."

In 2017, the AI cluster picked up a repeated irregularity in the dates of recorded satellite captures over the Nahanni Interior: **duplicate thermal anomalies recorded on different days** but at the exact same coordinates. One spike appeared on June 13. The second — with the same heat signature and terrain profile — appeared on June 9. No satellite errors. No clock drift. The anomaly arrived *before* it left.

The AI flagged it:
"Temporal conflict: directional inversion."

One Dene story, rarely shared outside ceremony, tells of "a ridge that walks backward through the moonlight." Those who climb it may return before they leave. Or not at all.

A modern trapper once described the same feeling after returning to base:
"I looked at my footprints in the snow. They were already there, heading out, before I'd even gone."

And sometimes, the people themselves return with different watches, unreadable journals, and memories out of sync with the rest of their group. Days pass in the wrong order. Equipment logs entries that no one remembers typing.

The Nahanni doesn't just resist maps.

Sometimes it **resets the timeline**.

And if you vanish in a place like that… you might return **before the reason you left**.

Chapter 25 – The Things That Left No Footprints

There had been snow on the ground for three days straight. A thick, fresh layer—not the patchy melt of late autumn or the shallow dust of a passing storm, but a full, silent snowfall that had buried everything from branch to stone. Perfect for tracking. Perfect for confirming movement. And yet—what we found had no tracks.

It was a campsite. Not old. Not ancient. No signs of decay. A recently burned fire ring, still rimmed with warm stones. A small aluminum cook pot sitting beside a half-finished meal. A compression bag from a sleeping roll partially unzipped, as if the owner had stepped away for a moment. There was even a pair of gloves drying on a branch over the fire ring, frozen stiff in a shape that suggested they'd been placed there only hours before.

But the snow was undisturbed.

No prints led to the site. None left it. Not even those faint drag patterns left by fabric or poles. Just a stillness. A kind of sterile, surgical calm that made it feel like the camp had been set down there, fully formed, by something that never touched the ground.

The wind hadn't shifted in days. There were no melt patterns from heat. No sign of animals. No tree branches broken or pressed down. Only the camp, like a memory caught in place. And that terrible, quiet fire ring—smudged in a way that suggested warmth had been present recently… but not human warmth.

We walked the perimeter five times. Measured our steps. Dropped trail markers. Tried to dismiss it. Maybe the prints had been covered. Maybe it was older than it looked. But no one believed that. Something had come here. And whatever it was, it didn't leave signs the way we do.

We packed up and left in silence.

By morning, the campsite was gone.

And there were our tracks leading right up to where it had been.
Nothing else.

Chapter 26 – The Ones Who Heard the Singing

It's always distant.
It never rushes.
And it never sounds quite **human**.

The first mention came from a 1921 prospector's journal, recovered posthumously from the base of First Canyon. A single entry near the back:
"Woman's voice. No words. Just melody. Moving between trees. Came from upslope. No one was there."

He fell to his death three days later. Officially ruled an accident.

The phenomenon has no formal classification, but local accounts use terms like *"hill music,"* *"fog voices,"* and *"the river's daughter."* One search-and-rescue operator called it simply: *"The Sound That Leads."*

It's not singing in the traditional sense.
There are no lyrics. No language. Just tones — long, soft, repeating. Sometimes single-voice. Sometimes layered, like a forgotten choir.

In 1978, a trapper near Deadmen Valley heard the sound for two consecutive nights. On the third, he followed it uphill. He returned at sunrise — disoriented, frostbitten, and silent for three full days. When he finally spoke, he described the voice as "too kind… like it knew what I wanted to hear."

In 1996, a solo kayaker was found after going missing for five days. His boat was intact. His gear, untouched. He claimed the voice had "sung the shape of the water" to him. He also claimed he hadn't eaten in three days — but his body showed **no signs of starvation**.

A particularly eerie report comes from a wildlife biologist in 2012. She was tagging caribou near The Curve when she heard it — a hum with melody, repeating four notes. She recorded it on her phone. Later analysis revealed no vocal frequency. Just **pulsed resonance** — a sonic signature more common to **deep ocean mammal calls** than anything terrestrial.

But the sound came from the trees.

And it was **following her**.

She refused to return the following season.

When the AI parsed all known acoustic anomalies in the Nahanni, the singing registered in three distinct frequency bands. One below human hearing. One within it. One **above**. That tripartite structure doesn't match any known vocal behavior — human or animal.

Even more disturbing: one incident from 2004 included a report from a deaf hiker who signed to his partner:
"Do you feel it singing?"

He hadn't heard it.

He'd **felt** it.

Among local Dene communities, there are old teachings about "the singing wind" — a force that comes not from above, but **from below**, carried upward through stone. Sometimes it mimics the voices of those lost. Other times… it calls in tones no one recognizes. Either way, the elders say the same thing:

"Do not answer."

Because once you do, it changes pitch.

And then it starts to move closer.

Chapter 27 – The Quiet Between the Pines

Silence in the wilderness is normal. Expected. It comes with snow, or windbreaks, or dusk. But in the Nahanni, there are zones where silence behaves differently — it arrives **with intent**.

They call it "the quiet between the pines."

The first formal report came in 1962 from a Parks Canada ranger describing a stretch of forest along the lower Flat River Trail. The log entry read:
"Birdsong stopped. Wind died. Felt wrong to step forward. As if I'd interrupted something."

He never filed another entry from that patrol. Later notes by his partner marked the incident as *"psychosomatic."*

But the pattern didn't stop.

In 1985, a group of backpackers passing through a dense pine corridor described "walking into cotton." Not fog — **sound**. One said his breathing went quiet. Another claimed the gravel underfoot stopped crunching. Their dog froze, ears flattened, then tried to bolt. It refused to re-enter the area for the remainder of the trip.

The silence, they noted, had weight.

The AI eventually flagged over 30 incidents of "auditory suppression zones" — places where individuals described near-total sensory muting. In 12 of those cases, travelers reported the same detail:
"The trees were listening."

In 2009, a fire watch drone crossed one such corridor. Audio sensors on board showed a measurable dip in ambient decibels — below baseline wilderness norms. One technician noted:
"The forest stopped. Even the insects."

No natural explanation was offered. The drone lost signal 4 minutes later and never reconnected.

Indigenous oral history offers a different lens. Among several Dene communities, there are stories of forest spaces where the land "goes still to hear better." These places are not evil — but they are watching. Moving through them is possible. Speaking in them is not advised.

In a particularly harrowing 1994 incident, a forestry worker reported entering a pine stand during a solo trek. He heard nothing — not even his own footfalls. When he spoke aloud to test the silence, he later claimed **his own voice came back to him… slightly altered.**

Lower. Slower.

And still speaking after his mouth had closed.

He never returned to the valley.

When asked why, he only said:
"It wasn't an echo. It was a reply."

What causes the Quiet? No one knows. It isn't tied to elevation, season, or weather. It happens in different zones — and rarely in the same place twice. But when it comes…

The birds stop.
The wind dies.
And if you stand too long in it, something **leans in to listen**.

Chapter 28 – They Never Found Their Own Camps

Getting lost in the bush is easy.
Losing your own camp when it's **within sight** is something else entirely.

The Nahanni has a long list of missing persons. But stranger still are the accounts from people who made it back — shaken, starved, and terrified — all repeating the same impossible sentence:

"I couldn't find my own camp."

In 1974, a wildlife researcher named Murray Greaves left his tent to collect water at dusk. The river was no more than 100 meters away. He followed a marked path — flagged earlier that day — and returned less than ten minutes later.

The tent was gone. So were the flags. So was the trail.

Greaves wandered for three days before stumbling upon his own camp **from the opposite direction**, as if the land had rotated while he was gone. His watch showed only 45 minutes had passed. His face was sunburnt. The food in his pack was spoiled.

In 1988, a young biologist on a tagging expedition radioed that she was hiking back to base camp after setting motion sensors. She never arrived. A week later, search crews found her tent, undisturbed. Inside was her gear, notes, and the original log she'd sent by radio.

But she was camped **just 300 meters from her original location** — unaware. Convinced she was dozens of kilometers away. She'd passed within 100 feet of her own tracks multiple times.

When asked why she hadn't recognized the terrain, she simply said:
"It wasn't the same place. It looked like the copy of somewhere I'd already been."

In 2003, two hunters exited their shelter in the early morning to scout a nearby ridge. When they returned an hour later, their tent was missing. Not stolen. Not scattered. Just... not there. No tracks. No gear. Just flat grass where it had stood.

They were found a day later, dehydrated, camped under a tarp — the only piece of shelter they carried in their packs. Their original camp was discovered over two kilometers upslope, in a clearing neither man recognized. But both swore they hadn't climbed.

The AI system, when fed these and similar cases, generated a chilling phrase in its summary clustering:

"Non-consensual displacement within static terrain."

The terrain didn't move.
The people didn't move.
And yet — they lost each other.

Dene folklore references a similar phenomenon: places where "the land wears a mask." Entering such a space is like walking into a memory that isn't yours. The stories warn: **"Tie something to yourself. If the land blinks, you might be standing in its dream."**

Perhaps the most haunting case involved a solo backpacker in 2017. His journal, recovered after a successful rescue, included a final entry written in trembling hand:

"I saw my own fire from the ridge. I walked toward it. I walked for hours. It never got closer."

He collapsed 80 meters from his unburned fire pit.

Chapter 29 – They Came Back Changed

Most never come back.

But the ones who do… are not quite who they were.

In 1982, a SAR crew recovered a man named Thomas Baird after he'd been missing for six days in a heavily wooded region near Glacier Lake. When they found him, he was seated on a flat rock, clothes torn, barefoot, staring straight ahead. His vitals were stable. His eyes didn't move.

When questioned, he said only:
"It wasn't a place. It was a voice that became a hallway."

He never explained further.

Baird was a licensed geologist with a sharp memory. Post-recovery, he forgot the names of his children. He couldn't identify the tools he'd used for twenty years. But he could recite — word for word — **a list of coordinates** that mapped directly onto an uninhabited quadrant of the valley, later flagged by the AI as a "signal suppression corridor."

He had never been there before his disappearance.

In 1999, two hunters emerged from the bush after being presumed dead for eleven days. They had water but no food. No explanation. Their GPS logs showed that they had hiked nearly 50 kilometers without knowing it. Both men were sunburned — but **only on the backs of their necks**. They reported no memory of sunlight.

One spoke of "gray sky music."
The other kept repeating: *"It watched us sleep."*

They both retired from the outdoors that year. One moved south and refused further interviews. The other, in a written statement, said:
"It didn't want to keep us. It wanted to mark us."

Medical reports sometimes note unusual aftereffects:
– Lowered body temperature, persistent for weeks
– Temporary aphasia (loss of speech)
– Disassociation from familiar places and people
– Sudden shifts in sleep cycle and circadian rhythm
– In one case, mild but **measurable changes in bone density**

These changes aren't consistent. But they occur too frequently to ignore.

Indigenous stories describe this, too. Not as punishment, but as **initiation**. The valley doesn't harm everyone who enters — some are chosen to carry something back. Not a message. Not even a memory.

A **resonance**.

There's a word among certain Dene storytellers:
Nágah shílé.
Roughly translated: *"The shape that walks out wearing your face."*

In modern terms, we might call it **subtle replacement** — not a body swap, not possession, but something more insidious: an imperceptible overlay. A shift in identity so quiet it passes for exhaustion.

The AI flagged only eight full cases of this phenomenon — but nearly forty partials. All clustered around zones with other anomalies: acoustic events, disappearances, fire signatures.

All involve one thing in common:
They came back.

And yet... those who knew them best often say:

"Not all of them did."

Chapter 30 – They Built Fires for the Wrong Reasons

Campfires are tools — ancient ones. Warmth, light, protection, signal. Every backcountry traveler knows when and where to use them. And when **not** to.

But in the Nahanni, fire doesn't always follow logic.

In dozens of incident reports — from missing persons, SAR rescues, and recovered journals — there are fires built **under conditions that made no sense**. Fires built in daylight. In oppressive heat. With no food present. In the rain. And, in the most unsettling cases… **alone**, in places where there were no confirmed survivors.

In 1965, a journal was recovered from a geologist who vanished near Hell's Gate. The final pages describe a series of "drifting lights" seen near the tree line. He built a fire — not to see, not to stay warm — but because "I felt like I had to mark myself. Like the fire would make me real again."

He was never found.

The journal was dry. The fire pit was still warm.

In 1987, a fire ranger on aerial patrol spotted a lone fire on a ledge not marked on any map. It was burning bright — visible for kilometers. No call for help was ever received. The coordinates were logged, but by the time a crew arrived 12 hours later, **there was no fire. No ash. No disturbed ground.**

The GPS tag from the plane matched with a spot that appeared **impossible to reach on foot**.

In 2002, a missing climber was recovered after three nights alone. He had a fire burning when rescuers found him — despite heavy rain. When asked how he lit it, he couldn't answer. Later, his sister reviewed his journal. One line stood out, written during his first night alone:
"I think they only see me when I burn."

Fire as signal.
Fire as ward.
Fire as **permission**.

The AI ran linguistic analyses on every known fire-related entry from Nahanni sources. It found an unusual repetition of phrases like *"keep them out,"* *"stay seen,"* *"make the circle,"* and most

notably:
"Don't let it go out."

One SAR worker in 2016 recovered a solo camp where the fire had been kept burning for five consecutive days. Bundled wood had been pre-staged in a perfect ring — as if the camper knew they wouldn't have time to gather more later.

There was no body. No blood. No sign of struggle. Just embers still hot… and a single phrase carved into bark:

"I didn't light it. I found it burning."

Local Dene legend warns against "false warmth" — fires that draw the wrong attention. Some say the valley can mimic comfort, and that those who build fires too easily are not lighting their own.

A modern hunter once said it this way:
"Sometimes a fire in Nahanni isn't a fire. It's a doorway. And sometimes… it swings inward."

Chapter 31 – The Coordinates You Shouldn't Say Out Loud

Some places vanish from maps. Others vanish from memory.

But the most dangerous are the ones that remain — **unspoken**.

Throughout the field notes, missing person reports, and recovered journals tied to the Nahanni, a pattern began to form. Not just overlapping locations — but repeated **coordinates**. Numbers. Precise. Deliberate. They don't appear often, and when they do, they're usually buried in margins, scribbled into gear logs, or whispered in audio recordings.

Never spoken twice.

In one 1973 RCMP report, a field investigator abruptly ended his summary after writing:
"All signs point to 61°17'24"N, 125°43'59"W — but I won't log that again."

He died of an aneurysm two months later. His file was reassigned.

That same coordinate resurfaced in 1986 in the notes of a hydrologist studying underground water anomalies. He had no access to the 1973 report. He called the site "unsettlingly dry." His final log entry, handwritten:
"The silence is different here. Like the numbers themselves are listening."

He deleted the GPS waypoint from his system. It was recovered manually later.

The AI model didn't flag the coordinates at first — not because they weren't anomalous, but because **they were too consistent**. Most geographic anomalies show drift. These didn't.

When asked to isolate all GPS points that appeared in more than two unrelated documents, the system paused for 6.3 seconds, then returned four.

Each matched known event clusters:
– A place where three solo travelers vanished in 1960
– A ridge where thermal distortion was detected for 23 minutes in 2005
– A valley floor where an animal tagging drone disappeared mid-flight
– And the glacial ledge where a hunter's last radio call was recorded… **hours before he entered the park**

What links these sites isn't just tragedy.

It's the behavior of people around them.

A SAR pilot who helped search two of the sites said:
"We never talk about those numbers. They're fine to write. But don't say them. It gets into your sleep."

In 2012, a park employee quit abruptly after logging an internal complaint that another staffer had "spoken the wrong coordinates out loud, twice." His resignation letter read:
"There are places you can't name. Not because they're secret. But because they aren't done listening."

One Dene elder was asked directly about one of the suspect coordinates. He didn't answer at first. Then he said:

"We don't give names to places that already have their own."

And when pressed:

"You keep your map quiet. Or the land draws one back on you."

We think of coordinates as fixed — lifeless — mere reference.
But in Nahanni, numbers aren't neutral.

Some of them… are watching to see who speaks them next.

Chapter 32 – What the Birds Refuse to Fly Over

Wilderness speaks in flight paths.

In most of North America, birds are reliable. They follow the weather, food sources, and generations-old migratory routes. Scientists model it. Satellites confirm it. It works.

Until you reach Nahanni.

Starting as early as the 1940s, bush pilots began noting strange aerial corridors — places where birds never appeared, even in peak migration. "Empty lanes," one called them. As if **carved through the sky.**

Some said it was coincidence. Others called it superstition. But by the 1980s, biologists began logging it more precisely: GPS-tagged geese, falcons, crows, and even ravens — all demonstrated sudden rerouting patterns over specific zones in the valley.

One 1983 banding study recorded a group of northern pintails that veered a full 8 kilometers east to avoid flying over an uninhabited basin. A second group — untagged but visible — followed the same evasive arc.

Weather was clear. Thermals were optimal.
There was no storm. No smoke. No terrain obstruction.

Just **avoidance**.

In 2009, a satellite imaging project tracked 117 migratory birds fitted with lightweight transponders. Of the 117, **19 flew direct paths across Nahanni**. The rest avoided a narrow 15km strip — most of them diverting with sharp, deliberate angles, then resuming their normal route once clear.

The AI flagged these as "avian aversion corridors."

What's more disturbing? One of the avoidance zones corresponds **exactly** with three missing-person clusters, two known auditory anomalies, and one of the black-sky photographic failures from the 1960s.

A 2015 drone-mounted acoustic array noted another strange metric: in these zones, **birdsong drops to zero**, even from the perimeter. Microphones detect the approach of avian sound — and then **nothing**. As if the silence begins before the birds even reach the border.

Locals had noticed long before the tech did.

Dene elders speak of "skyholes" — spaces not of emptiness, but **fullness**. Places where flight is unwelcome. One elder said:
"They don't go because something already flew there once... and never came down."

An old trapper from Nahanni Butte described watching a hawk catch a strong updraft — only to stop mid-air, flap once, then turn around and flee, crying out. He never saw it again.

Migratory birds are deeply attuned to magnetic fields, subtle air pressure, and acoustic resonance far beyond human perception. What they're avoiding isn't just a shape. It's a **presence**.

Maybe it's sound we can't hear.
Or pressure we can't measure.
Or maybe... it's memory.

Whatever the cause, the result is clear:

There are places in Nahanni where **even the sky avoids looking down**.

And if the birds — who cross thousands of miles on instinct alone — are too afraid to fly overhead...

We should ask why.

Chapter 33 – The Ledge That Isn't On the Map

It overlooks nothing.

No waterfall. No canyon. No scenic drop. Just a sharp, narrow shelf of exposed limestone halfway up a pine-choked ridge. Flat. Unnatural. And — according to maps dating back a century — completely nonexistent.

And yet, it keeps showing up.
In photos that won't geotag.
In eyewitness accounts that never match coordinates.
In the dreams of people who've never been to Nahanni.

The first confirmed sighting was recorded in 1951 by a hiker named Abigail Wren. Her journal mentions "a gray lip of rock, halfway up the ridge — dry as bone, warm to the touch." She described standing on it for several minutes before hearing what she called a "distant static breath." She left immediately. Her sketch of the area is detailed.

No such ledge exists at those coordinates.

A decade later, in 1963, a botanist named Lambert spotted a shelf matching her description. He hiked toward it, but it vanished behind the trees. When he reached the slope, he found nothing. The GPS he carried later reset itself to factory default. His analog altimeter showed a sudden 700-foot gain — in level terrain.

In 1990, two climbers set up base near a ridge known for bighorn sightings. From their tent, they could see the ledge clearly through binoculars. One described a sensation of "being watched by something beneath the stone." They hiked out the next morning. On review of their footage, the ledge was visible in two frames — then vanished from the sequence entirely. **Not blurred. Not distant. Gone.**

The AI pattern system was fed dozens of instances like these and attempted to triangulate a location.

Its result:
"Undefined fixed feature. High stability. No spatial persistence."

The AI had never before described something as **fixed and impermanent** at the same time.

In one particularly strange case, a search-and-rescue team attempting to reach a suspected vantage point above Deadmen Valley marked their GPS at the summit. When they returned two hours later, the same route took them to **a completely different terrain face**. They repeated the hike twice, each time arriving somewhere new.

One team member insisted:
"The ledge moves."

Dene oral history references a high place known simply as *Tłon Dehá* — loosely translated: **"The edge that watches from inside."**

It is not sacred. It is not cursed.
It is **avoided**.

They say those who stand on it too long report sudden changes in memory — names misplaced, faces forgotten, emotions tied to places they haven't visited yet. Some descend and cannot remember *which direction they came from.*

In the notes of a 2004 geospatial intern analyzing ridge-line aerials, one line was underlined twice:

"The ledge exists only when no one is recording it."

Chapter 34 – The Trail Markers That Change

A red cloth. A scratched X on a birch. Cairns stacked three high. Plastic tape fluttering from a branch.

Trail markers are the wilderness traveler's handshake — simple, honest, human. They're how we speak to ourselves on the way back. Proof we've been here before. Signposts for return.

But in the Nahanni, they **don't stay put.**

In one 1975 incident, a solo tracker named Jean Rowe used reflective tacks to mark her route into a narrow gulley system north of First Canyon. She placed the markers at shoulder height, spaced every 50 meters. She kept count. Seventeen in total.

When she turned around six hours later, she found only five.

Four were removed entirely. Eight were relocated — now forming **a straight line leading in a different direction**, down into thicker forest. The final marker was embedded in a stump 10 feet off the ground.

Rowe didn't finish the loop. She was airlifted out the next day, shaking and mute.

She never camped solo again.

SAR teams have reported similar events: GPS-logged flagging tape found missing within hours. Marker stacks shifted overnight. Bright orange trail ribbons found tied **in knots** — or worse, in **symbols**. One was twisted into a shape resembling a spiral with a jagged tail. A linguist consulted later said it resembled "a directional ideogram, but to nowhere."

In 2001, a researcher returned to a familiar area marked with durable stone cairns. What she found chilled her: the cairns were still there — same number, same rocks — but now **reversed in order**, like someone had **rewound her route**.

The AI, when given these accounts alongside satellite metadata, offered a chilling suggestion:

"User-placed markers altered by unknown agency. Behavioral consistency implies intent."

Intent.

Not weather. Not wildlife.
Something watching the trail… and choosing to answer.

In Dene stories, there are whispers of a forest shape called *Nah dáré'* — "the mimic hand." It moves like us, copies like us, but not to understand. It marks differently, subtly. One degree at a time.

An elder once said:
"If your markers are not how you left them, someone has walked with you."

The worst reports come from those who *trust* their markers and follow them. In at least four disappearances from 1988 to 2015, the final known action of the missing person was **doubling back to check a moved marker**.

Some SAR members now follow an unspoken rule:
If a marker looks wrong, **ignore it.**
If it leads somewhere unfamiliar, **go the other way.**

One man, interviewed in 2019 after his rescue, said it best:
"I kept putting up tape. It kept vanishing. So I stopped marking. And that's when I found the way out."

Chapter 35 – When the Maps Disagree with the Ground

Maps are promises. They tell us what's coming, where we've been, and how far it is to get back. They mark danger. They imply logic. They offer trust.

But in Nahanni... they lie.

More accurately: **they no longer apply.**

Over decades of field notes, GPS logs, topographic comparisons, and even satellite overlays, one pattern repeats: what the maps say **should be there** — isn't. And what appears underfoot **shouldn't be possible.**

In 1972, a geological survey crew documented a glacial runoff trail just north of Broken Skull River. Three weeks later, a second team using the same charts and GPS coordinates found no such trail — just dense, mature black spruce. No erosion. No stones. No streambed. The first crew's photos were dismissed as mislocation.

But the sky in the photos? **Matches the exact forecast** on that date. It wasn't a mistake.

In 1994, a SAR team attempting to retrace a lost hiker's path discovered a mismatch between their topo and the terrain. A ravine marked as "minor, crossable" had transformed into a 20-foot drop with sheer slickrock. Their team lead, an experienced mapper, refused to camp near the site, saying:
"This place doesn't know it was drawn."

By 2010, the problem had gone digital. Satellite-based platforms began to show **terrain drift** in certain parts of the valley — as if elevation lines warped slightly when re-rendered across seasons. One heatmap revealed land masses that moved **hundreds of meters laterally** compared to their charted position just two years earlier.

The AI's analysis was blunt:
"Local cartography degrades at variable intervals. Recalibration ineffective. Root cause: undefined."

Not user error.
Not magnetic anomalies.
Something deeper. Something **unmappable**.

Local bush pilots have long known this intuitively. Many keep their **own hand-drawn maps** in the cockpit — versions that contradict the official ones. A few have marked spots with notes like:
– *"Too deep. Doesn't match."*
– *"This ridge moved."*
– *"Can't see what should be here."*

One pilot — now retired — spoke candidly:
"The river changes sides. That's the only way I can describe it. One season, you bank left to follow it. The next, it curves right — and always has. The ground rewrites the memory."

Among Dene storytellers, there are tales of "sleeping land" — terrain that **wakes only when walked**, and **closes when left behind**. The valley, they say, only lets you **map the parts that are watching back**.

It's no surprise then, that a handful of recovered journals contain drawings of territory that do not match any known contour. But what's worse: **the drawings match each other.** Made by different people, in different years, with no access to each other's notes.

Identical.
And all of them wrong.

Or…
All of them true **only when you're there.**

Chapter 36 – The Tribe That Walked Into the Valley

Long before maps, surveys, or chartered airspace, the Nahanni Valley was known by another name:

Dehé T'áhgot'į — "The River With Teeth."

Among the Dene, the land is not owned. It is respected. And feared. Stories passed down through generations carry warnings — not parables, but **event memory**. One story above all reappears, in variations across clans, languages, and river systems:

A tribe entered the valley.
Armed. Angry.
They never came out.

The most consistent form of the story tells of a **hostile party** — sometimes a full band of warriors, sometimes an entire tribe seeking conquest — crossing into Nahanni. Some were fleeing. Others chasing. But all were warned.

And none were seen again.

In one telling, passed down from the Mountain Dene, a war band pursued fugitives into the valley. Days passed. Scouts vanished. Their fires turned cold. The last signal was smoke seen above the treetops — **a perfect black column, rising unnaturally straight**, then disappearing. The pursuing tribe was never heard from again.

Centuries later, these stories echoed in colonial encounters.

In 1908, a prospector named Harry McLeod wrote in his journal:
"The Indians say the valley is where a nation went to war with the land… and the land won."

He dismissed it as superstition.
He was found dead two years later — **beheaded** — along the Flat River.

Another version of the legend describes **songs echoing** out of the mountains after the war party vanished. But they weren't Dene songs. They were… *something else*. One elder said:
"The land swallowed their names. What came out singing wasn't them."

AI pattern analysis found something curious: a cluster of modern disappearances — between 1935 and 1970 — that occurred in a tight radius matching the oldest legends. The common denominator? **Groups of three or more**, usually moving fast, ignoring caution, or on a mission.

All were reported as confident. None left trace.

It's as if the valley doesn't merely **consume the hostile** — it **removes the impatient**. The ones who believe it is something to conquer.

One researcher once theorized the legend as "a cultural ghost story" meant to reinforce territorial boundaries. But that doesn't explain the **synchronous disappearances**, the matching details, the sheer silence where noise should remain.

One Dene elder, when asked about the story, replied with something older than myth.
Not a warning.
Not a parable.
A sentence that felt like a fact:

"They went where names don't echo."

Chapter 37 – The Mammoth Trail and the Warm Ground

The first time the word *"mammoth"* appeared in connection with Nahanni was in 1898 — scribbled in the margins of a fur trapper's log. He was describing large, round tracks found near a thermal spring system well beyond any trail.

He didn't say *it was* a mammoth.
He said:
"If the old books are true, this is where they went to hide."

Over the next century, that idea — impossible as it is — kept resurfacing.

Hair-covered shapes.
Low thunderous calls echoing through valleys in the night.
Massive bone fragments "too heavy to carry," never found again.

Most accounts were secondhand, passed over campfires or through bush radio chatter. But some came from men who had no interest in fantasy: hydrologists, game wardens, a helicopter crew who swore they saw **movement** in an isolated, green pocket during a winter survey.

The AI processed over 2,400 documents tied to the valley and flagged 34 as "descriptions of anachronistic megafauna." Of those, **17 referenced heat**, vegetation, or thawed terrain **in areas that should be subarctic permafrost.**

These were not YouTube claims or conspiracy blogs.
They came from typed incident logs, aerial scans, and declassified geology briefs.

And then there's the **vegetation**.

In a 1981 Canadian Wildlife Service memo (retrieved via FOI request), a biologist references **broadleaf plant growth** in an uncharted sector east of Sunblood Mountain — plants normally found hundreds of kilometers south. The memo concludes:
"Suggest geothermal activity localized to a microclimate pocket. Further investigation deferred."

It never happened.

Local First Nations stories include whispers of warm ground and old giants. One elder told of a place "where breath does not frost and trees grow in winter." Another referenced "**the beasts that do not forget the snow**", still walking **deep in the breathing ground**.

In 2004, a wildlife photographer hiking solo captured a distant image: a blurred mass on a low ridge. The frame is poor — heat shimmer, poor contrast. But scale estimates put the object at 3.4 meters tall, humped, and covered in reddish-brown.

She never released the full series.
She did, however, move to Yellowknife and refused all interviews.

Satellite thermal overlays in 2016 picked up **non-conforming heat signatures** along the base of a deep glacial fracture. When an unmanned drone attempted a scan, it crashed within 200 meters. The logs were corrupted. The backup was wiped.

The file remains under review.

What if the valley **never froze completely**?
What if, like a lung held in stone, it **exhaled slowly**, keeping a small pocket warm enough to hold life that should have vanished?

Maybe it's myth.
Maybe it's memory.
Maybe — in the deepest folds of Nahanni — the past isn't gone. It's just **waiting for the ice to thin.**

Chapter 38 – They Left Notes They Didn't Write

The valley doesn't echo. It replies.

Over the decades, field teams have recovered scattered fragments from missing hikers, researchers, and hunters. Notebook pages tucked in plastic sleeves. Handwritten scrawls on the backs of maps. Margin notes on gear checklists. Sometimes, they're found in abandoned camps. Sometimes, buried in rocks. A few are found with the bodies.

But the strangest are the ones that appear where **no one had been** — and say things their authors couldn't have known.

In 1979, the journal of botanist Caleb Foran was found under a cairn six kilometers from his last known location. Inside were sketches of local flora, consistent with his work. But toward the back, he had written:

"The breathing stopped today. I don't remember what it belonged to."

His handwriting was verified. But the page was dated **three days after his death**.

In 1995, SAR crews recovered a hunter's notebook from a drybag caught in a tree — 40 feet up. Most of the notes were mundane: gear, weather, meals. But one line stood out:

"Don't believe the map when the sky is wrong."

His sister, also an avid outdoorswoman, confirmed:
"That's not how he spoke. And he never used phrases like that. He didn't write like that."

The AI pattern analysis flagged dozens of such entries across 40 years. Some contained **geological data** the authors couldn't have known. Others referenced landmarks only visible from aerial views — at a time before drones or flyovers.

Some notes seem to reference **encounters** the authors never lived to report.
And in a few chilling cases… references to **themselves** in third-person:

– *"He doesn't know what he followed."*
– *"She thought the fire would keep her safe. It didn't."*
– *"I left, but the part of me that stayed behind still writes."*

In one case, a slip of paper recovered from a dry cave bore no name, but DNA analysis later confirmed it came from a hiker who'd been declared missing ten years earlier. The message read:

"If you're reading this, then it likes you."

Among the Dene, there is an idea not of possession, but of **"shared name"** — where something in the land **learns a person** so intimately it can mimic their memory, their cadence, their thought. The being is not a copy. It is a **continuation without consent**.

One elder said:
"Some places keep your story going even after you stop telling it."

When shown the final pages of one such journal, the AI flagged 11 phrases as non-correlated with any of the author's previous writing. Five matched prior case reports.

Two matched **entries from other missing persons' journals**, written decades apart.

Whatever leaves the messages… **knows the others**.

And if these notes weren't written by their owners…
Then who — or **what** — is still writing?

Chapter 39 – When the Silence Starts to Follow You

The wilderness is never truly quiet.

Wind threads through pine. Birds call warnings. Insects hum under moss. The river speaks. Even solitude in the backcountry carries sound — a natural rhythm that settles into the bones of anyone who's lived in it long enough.

But in Nahanni, there are places where **that rhythm dies**.
Not muffled. Not absorbed. **Withdrawn.**

The first mention of "following silence" comes from a 1962 geological survey. A technician working a solo ridge line reported a moment where **all noise simply ended.** No wind. No birds. Not even the hum of his own breath in his ears.

He moved. The silence followed.

He described it as a **"weight behind the air."** His report was never filed officially — just a margin note in a topographic log:
"Whatever's back there doesn't make sound. It takes it."

The AI combed through 77 reports from Nahanni that mention variations of "unnatural quiet," "sound dropped out," or "too still." In 41 cases, the silence was described as **mobile** — shifting with the subject, like a presence **hovering just out of view.**

Some said it stayed behind them.
Others felt it wrap around their ears — as if the **land was listening so intently it forgot to breathe.**

In 2003, a solo canoeist felt the silence begin around Flat River. His satellite beacon logged his position. No emergency was triggered. But his last journal entry reads:

"It's not that I can't hear. It's that nothing wants to make sound anymore. It's watching now. From the hush."

He was never found. His paddle was recovered — snapped cleanly in half, both pieces upright in the river mud, **pointing downstream.**

Acoustic specialists working with SAR drones over the valley have noted dead zones — places where **recordings return as blank**. No static. No hiss. Just pure digital null. When the same drones are flown elsewhere, their systems resume normally.

The AI labeled it **"non-environmental suppression."** Meaning:
It's not the trees.
Not the rock.
Not the wind.

Something is choosing silence.

One tracker, recovered from a 5-day missing event near Ram Head, said it plainly during debrief:

"It started out peaceful. Then it got quiet. Then it started walking behind me."

He refused to reenter the park.
He also no longer trusts the sound of his own footsteps — convinced some of them, even now, **aren't his.**

The Dene speak of a phenomenon called *Daałí ts'egha* — "The Quiet with Eyes." It's not evil. It's not kind. It simply *is*. A presence that watches through silence. Some say it's the valley dreaming. Others say it's the thing that *remains when the dreaming stops*.

One elder, when asked directly, said:

"When the sound goes, it's not gone. It's listening to what you do without it."

Chapter 40 – The Fires That No One Claimed

Fire should always mean someone's nearby.

In wilderness regions like the Nahanni, smoke is a signal — camp, cooking, rescue, danger. It's human. It's explainable. It means **someone else is out there.**

But in Nahanni, there are fires that no one admits to starting.
And worse — **fires that don't leave anything behind.**

In 1937, a bush pilot flying low along the Ragged Range spotted two fires burning just below tree line. Both burned steady and small — isolated, no wind spread. When rangers arrived 36 hours later, there were no signs of fire damage. No ash. No burn radius. Not even scorched moss.

The official report concluded: **"Likely heat shimmer or reflection."**
But the pilot insisted:
"Those were cook fires. Neatly built. Clean. Like someone knew we'd be watching."

Over the next 80 years, dozens of similar accounts surfaced:

- Thin smoke rising from ridgelines that later prove untouched.

- Flame seen through trees from kilometers away — too small to be wild, too large to be a cigarette.

- Infrared sensors on flyovers detecting brief, high-heat blooms... then nothing.

The AI review found 54 separate references to "unclaimed fires" across 13 independent data sources. In 22 cases, SAR or research teams attempted to investigate within 24 hours. In every case: **no evidence** of flame, heat, or combustion.

And still, the fire is seen.
Sometimes at night.
Sometimes more than once in the same place.

In 2002, a documentary crew attempting to film nocturnal wildlife spotted a flickering glow through the trees. Thinking it was another group, they moved toward it. After an hour of hiking, the fire **seemed farther away**. They gave up.

The next morning, they realized their tracks had arced **in a perfect circle**, leading them back to their own camp.

Their map pins had not moved. But their direction had.
And whatever flame they chased — **was never there to be caught**.

Indigenous stories sometimes reference "the hungry flame," or *Ts'edeh goné'*, which means roughly: **"the fire that asks nothing."** It does not warm. It does not destroy. It simply **burns in the wrong places**.

One elder explained it like this:

"If you see a fire where no one should be, it's not there for you. It's there for someone else. Someone long gone. Or someone not yet returned."

In one modern case, SAR radio logs recorded a fire spotted on the far side of a ridge at dusk. The crew split. Half reached the ridge. The other half saw the fire move — **sliding across the trees like it had feet.**

It vanished.

Thermal scans of the area registered **a human body temperature** — 98.6°F — hovering two meters above the ground.
For thirteen seconds.
Then it blinked out.

Fire has always meant presence. Life. Story.
But in the Nahanni…

There are fires that burn for no one.
And whatever they were meant to signal, we weren't the intended audience.

Chapter 41 – The Camps Found with Everything But the People

It's the food that stays warm that gets to you.

Not the empty tents. Not the boots still laced. Not the journals open to half-written entries. It's the stew still warm in the pot. The kettle placed neatly beside the fire. The sleeping bag peeled open like someone had just stepped out.

Nahanni doesn't just take people.
It leaves everything else **behind**.

The most infamous case was the **1906 disappearance of the MacLeod brothers**. Their camp was found deep upriver — fire cold, gear untouched, gold still packed in their bags. Both men were gone. Days later, one skull was found downstream.
No body. No signs of animal attack.
Just a clean, deliberate decapitation.

Since then, similar scenes have repeated:

In 1971, a three-person climbing team failed to check in. When the search party found their camp, **nothing was missing**. Gear was dry. Ropes coiled. Climbing harnesses neatly stowed. One of the tents had a zipper half-open. Inside: a journal entry that simply read:

"Something changed during the night."

No sign of the climbers has ever been found.

The AI, cross-referencing 118 disappearance reports and 34 SAR logs, identified a chilling commonality: in nearly 60% of the documented Nahanni vanishings, **camp was left in perfect order**.
Food not scavenged.
Tents not collapsed.
Clothes still folded.

More disturbing: in a subset of these cases, items that should have degraded — paper, plastic wrappers, fuel canisters — remained **pristinely preserved** even years later. It's as if the land respects what's left… but **not who left it.**

In 2008, a biologist's solo camp was found two weeks after he missed a check-in. His GPS was in standby mode. His boots were at the edge of the water. His backpack — fully packed — leaned gently against a tree. Inside, he had written:

"The silence tapped me on the shoulder."

In Dene oral tradition, this phenomenon is not new.
Some camps, they say, are **"opened by the land"**, prepared like altars. Not offerings to the valley — **but by the valley.**

One elder put it bluntly:

"When the people go missing, it's not their gear the valley wants. It's their path. Their choice. Their direction. It takes that. It erases it. The camp stays so you remember they were real."

Another SAR member described a 2016 scene: a firepit still warm, socks drying on a stick, and a radio playing static. The hiker was never found. The only sound left?

A voice on the tape recorder, whispering — "I'm not alone."

Was it the hiker's? No voice ID match was ever confirmed.

Was it an echo? A loop?
Or was it a reply?

Chapter 42 – They Marked Trees That Were Already Marked

Blazing a trail is survival.
It's how you say: "I was here. I will return."

From carved initials to ribbon tape, bent branches to stone cairns, humans leave signs for themselves — anchors in a land that shifts underfoot. In the Nahanni, many have tried. But more than once, they've discovered this truth:

The trees were already marked.

In 1954, a wildlife researcher began tagging spruce in a crescent pattern as he mapped migration paths near Vampire Peaks. After five days, he realized he was **re-blazing the same trees** — exact same placement, same depth, even identical gouge angles. He checked his logbook: these were trees **he hadn't reached yet**.

He left the valley early.

In 1989, two park rangers set up a new trail to reroute foot traffic away from a known avalanche zone. Three kilometers in, they noticed subtle, deliberate axe marks on certain trunks — **slanted at eye level**, facing north. They assumed old forestry blazes. But records showed no previous trails there, and no fire activity.

A month later, a fire did come — but **it skipped those trees.**

When AI was trained on ranger and SAR reports involving tree markings, it flagged an anomaly: 12 independent cases where **modern trail markers were found already duplicated** — sometimes exactly, sometimes *eerily close* — by unrecorded, unknown sources.

In one case, a GPS-tagged line of biodegradable tape was set along a ravine route. When the team returned two days later, the **same color tape** was visible on trees **ahead** of their path — tied with the same number of knots. But they hadn't gone that far yet.

Someone — or **something** — had marked the route in advance.

Or worse: the route **was remembering itself.**

Among Dene elders, this phenomenon is sometimes explained with the phrase:
"Náhłı̨ dúu káde" — "The trail folds back."

It means more than just a loop. It implies a **memory in the land itself**, a sort of **awareness of paths** — the idea that **some places anticipate your trail before you even choose it.**

One elder said:
"You think you're the first. The trees already knew you were coming."

Some of the marks aren't just familiar — they're **identical**.

A SAR lead in 2017 found a series of red spray paint arrows pointing the way out of a tangled ridge line. He followed them. They brought him back to the start. When he turned around, **the arrows had vanished.**
But days later, **his own paint can was empty.**
He'd used it. Just not when he thought he had.

What does it mean when the land responds before we act?
When the marks we use to navigate are already **waiting for us**?

In one final account from 2005, a cartographer flagged a tree deep in the valley with an aluminum tag stamped **"Survey Line A."**
Weeks later, a second team found another tree, five miles east, marked with the same tag number.

But they had **never received a second tag.**

And the metal was **weathered — like it had been there for years.**

Chapter 43 – The Warnings in the Wind

There is wind in the Nahanni, but it doesn't always behave like weather.

It doesn't follow terrain.
It doesn't match the forecast.
And sometimes — it feels like **it waits**.

In 1976, a group of hydrologists camped along the Flat River noticed a persistent gust blowing against their tents from the **north**, despite valley geography that funneled air consistently **from the west**. It began at dusk. It ended at sunrise. The same pattern continued for three nights.

On the fourth night, it stopped.
That was the night they heard **something large moving through the brush**, just outside the tent line.
Their gear was untouched. Their notes were gone.

They left the next morning, leaving behind most of their equipment. In a later interview, one researcher said:
"It wasn't the wind itself. It was what it stopped us from hearing."

The AI model cross-referenced wind speed, direction, and environmental logs with human disappearance reports. A correlation emerged: in over 60% of cases where the **last known location was confidently pinned**, witnesses reported **sudden wind changes** just before the person vanished.

Not storms.
Just abrupt shifts in pressure and tone — often followed by silence.

In 1993, a search-and-rescue tracker described feeling a "wall of moving air" that hit him **without sound**. He dropped his pack. His radio hissed once, then cut out. Ten minutes later, they found the missing hiker's coat — folded on a stump, twenty feet from the trail.

Another SAR member described it this way:

"It's like someone exhales right behind your head. You turn around — no one's there. But now you're off the path. Every time."

Bush pilots have long respected a particular ridge near Deadmen Valley where wind "refuses to rise." Even when gusts sweep the surrounding peaks, the ridge remains dead still — as if **the valley has pressed a finger to its lips.**

Indigenous stories from the region are clear on this:
The wind doesn't always belong to the sky.
Sometimes, it's the voice of the **land itself**.

One Dene story speaks of *Tłįchoa'ehda*, "the Listening Breath." It's not a spirit, not quite — more a **sentience that moves with the air**. It doesn't speak words. It speaks **removal**: a sudden gust when you ask the wrong question. A stall in the breeze when you near the wrong place.

Another tale describes an elder who turned back from a hunting trip after a "stillness in the wrong direction." Days later, a rockslide buried the trail he would've used.
His explanation?
"The wind said no."

In the Nahanni, listening to the wind is more than folklore. It's survival.

One recovered journal from 1988 includes this chilling line:

"The trees didn't warn me. The wind tried."

Chapter 45 – The Screaming That Wasn't Heard By Everyone

The human scream is unmistakable.

Whether it's pain, panic, or rage, it cuts through distance and fear alike. It demands response. But in the Nahanni, **the scream doesn't always reach everyone.**

One of the earliest references dates back to 1924, when a surveyor's log recorded "an echo with a human edge" heard at dusk near the Ram Range. He and his partner disagreed. He insisted someone cried out. His partner heard only wind.

Since then, dozens of similar cases have emerged — pairs, trios, entire teams where **only certain members hear a scream**. Always distant. Always chilling. And never from a direction that makes sense.

In 1981, a wildlife biologist hiking near Hell's Gate froze on the trail. He claimed to hear a child screaming — not once, but in **a repeated burst**, like it was stuck in a loop. His partner walking 10 feet ahead turned and said,
"What scream?"

The audio recorder clipped to his chest caught only ambient wind. But his vitals spiked — heart rate, adrenaline, respiration. A stress response consistent with hearing **something primal**.

In 2007, a park employee on an aerial flyover began panicking mid-flight. She insisted there was a scream coming through the headset — **not over radio**, but as if the plane itself was making the noise. The pilot and copilot heard nothing. The moment the headset was removed, the noise stopped. Her hearing returned to normal.

In each case, there was no commonality in distance, time of day, weather, or equipment. The only pattern was this: the scream always came **just before something changed.**

– A hiker gets lost.
– A guide turns around.
– A decision is reversed.

Almost as if it's a **warning**, but one **not meant for everyone**.

The AI flagged these anomalies under a unique tag:
"Differential Perception Clusters."

In its analysis, over 70% of these selective-auditory events were experienced by individuals who later **left the field early**, suffered equipment failure, or **went missing.** The ones who heard the scream often didn't survive long enough to report it — unless they turned back.

One recovered hiker described it like this:

"It sounded like something was being pulled apart. I looked at my friend — nothing on his face. He was still walking. I don't know how he didn't feel it. It wasn't just sound. It went through me."

Indigenous accounts refer to this as **Díę nedáhtı**, or *"the sound that chooses."* It doesn't aim to scare. It aims to **divide** — to separate the ones who hear from the ones who don't.

An elder described it plainly:

"If the land wants you to turn around, it tells you. Not everyone gets the message."

And some screams don't sound human.

One SAR team in 2014 logged an event where two members dove for cover, convinced an animal or man was wailing from the treeline. The third, standing between them, **heard nothing.**
Audio logs from their helmet mics?
Two picked up faint background distortion.
The third? Clear as day:

A scream.
Low. Drawn out.
And **too close to match any visible terrain.**

Chapter 46 – The Lights That Don't Illuminate

Out here, light is survival.

Campfires. Headlamps. The rising sun. Every flicker is a reassurance: you can still see, still orient, still fight off what waits in the dark.

But in Nahanni, some lights **don't help**.
They don't push the darkness back.
They simply exist within it — **and do not explain themselves.**

One of the earliest mentions dates to 1907. A trapper named Ellis Corman, deep in the upper South Nahanni watershed, wrote in his journal:

"Saw light near east slope. Bright, white. Thought was moon reflecting off snow. But light moved. Stopped. Stayed. Trees did not cast shadows."

His journal was found. His body was not.

In 1974, a bush pilot noted a strange glow hovering over the river. He circled back. Still there. No movement. No fire. No heat bloom on his sensors. It lit the surrounding mist, but not the trees below it. His cockpit camera jammed for precisely 43 seconds — the duration of the sighting.

Modern sightings are just as baffling.

SAR teams have reported **pale orbs**, stationary and silent, about the size of a grapefruit. When approached, they don't flicker. They **recede** — not flying away, but simply **not being where they were**. As if location is optional.

Hikers have followed lights, believing them to be other camps — only to arrive at a clearing with no fire, no ash, no footprints.

The AI identified over 90 references to anomalous lights in Nahanni-related logs, stretching from 1921 to 2023. Of these:

- 36 were described as **"cold light"** — no warmth, no radiant heat.

- 22 were reported in **complete fog**, yet somehow still visible.

- 17 caused **equipment failure**, from compasses spinning to batteries draining.

Most disturbing: 11 of these were **not visible to all witnesses present.**
One would see it. The others… nothing.

A 2011 field technician described it best:

"It wasn't lighting the area. It was lighting itself. Like the glow wasn't meant to help me — it was for something else."

Indigenous oral tradition speaks of **"lights that walk without fire"** — often associated with **portals**, spirits, or **ancient watchers**. Some tribes avoided entire valleys where such lights were known to appear. The lights weren't feared as monsters, but as **sentences waiting to be read.**

One Dene elder said:

"They are not there for you. They are not lost. They are not looking for a place to land. They are reminders. But of what, no one remembers."

One final report, found in a private notebook of a solo hiker who disappeared in 2018, included a sketch of a glowing ring in the treetops. The caption?

"Not a light. A hole where light came out."

Chapter 47 – The Tracks That Went Up the Cliff Face

Tracks tell a story.
They show pressure, direction, stride.
They prove someone was there — and where they went.

But in Nahanni, some tracks don't follow the rules.
They don't follow gravity.
Or terrain.
Or even **sense.**

The earliest known account came from a 1911 prospector's diary, discovered in a rusted lockbox. In a passage beneath a hand-drawn map of the valley's southwest quadrant, he wrote:

"Found tracks leading to base of limestone cliff. Deep. Barefoot. Continued upward across stone. No sign of handholds. Not animal. Not man."

He never named the cliff.
No corresponding bones or campsite were found.
But his sketch included a final note: **"Too long between steps."**

Decades later, multiple SAR teams began independently reporting "terminated tracks" — paths that lead into rock walls, over exposed ridgelines, or up vertical inclines, with **no visible transition.** Some suggest snow melt, optical illusion, or runoff erosion. But the most disturbing cases involve **dry terrain** and **fresh prints.**

One of the best-documented incidents occurred in 1984, when a search party followed a solo hiker's tracks to the base of a granite outcrop. The boot impressions were crisp — leading directly to the cliff face. And then: they continued **up**, climbing **12 feet vertically** before vanishing mid-surface. No rope. No scrape. No blood.
Just absence.

The AI classified these cases under **"ascent anomalies."** Of the 38 logs retrieved:

- 24 involved **barefoot or partial-foot impressions**, many in snow or moss.

- 9 included **clawlike or heel-less prints**, inconsistent with known fauna.

- 13 were verified by two or more independent parties.

- 6 were photographed. None of the negatives survived handling.

In 2006, a climber documented a line of depressions up a 40-degree shale incline. He photographed them. Later, when revisiting the site with a ranger, the prints were **gone** — not eroded or trampled. Just… not there.

He reviewed the photographs that evening.
The prints weren't in the images either.
But he remembers taking them.

One SAR technician described it as **"tracking something that changed its mind about being physical."**

In oral Dene traditions, this kind of event is tied to the concept of **"Skyfoot"** — not a being, but a *condition*, where something walks without needing the earth to hold it. It is said the land occasionally **lends form to memory**, and **not all memory needs gravity.**

Another elder, when told of vertical tracks leading into stone, responded with a quiet certainty:

"That's not them climbing. That's the land letting them go back."

In one particularly chilling modern case, drone footage captured what appeared to be **pressure indentations in moss**, ascending a boulder slope. The footage glitches for two seconds. When the video resumes, the tracks are still there — but now they **lead back down.**

No one saw what made them.

Chapter 48 – The Path That Wasn't on the Satellite Image Yesterday

Satellite imagery is supposed to be reliable.
It's machine-confirmed, timestamped, objective.
And in a place like the Nahanni — where boots fail, batteries die, and compasses drift — having the sky looking down **should** offer something solid.

But what happens when **the ground disagrees with the sky**?

In 2010, a survey team reviewing satellite passes over the Moose Ponds sector noticed something strange: a perfectly linear clearing, roughly 1.2 meters wide, winding through dense forest. Not fire-scorched. Not storm-cleared. Just open ground — like a footpath **etched in straight lines.**

It didn't appear in the imagery from the day before.
Nor did it appear again, two days later.
But the team that investigated found the path. **On foot.**

It was there. Real. Dirt worn smooth. Moss flattened. A visible trail.

And it led nowhere.

They flagged it, logged it, and turned back.
A month later, a second satellite pass showed **no disturbance** in the vegetation. As if the forest had never been opened. As if the trail had **never existed at all.**

The AI flagged similar reports stretching back to 1973 — long before drones or remote sensing. Researchers called them "ghost tracks" — trails that appear between visits, or are walked in-person but **don't show up on maps or aerial photos**, even those taken simultaneously.

In total:

- 19 cases included GPS-tagged coordinates of missing or inconsistent trails.

- 7 were verified by both aerial and on-ground personnel — with conflicting results.

- 5 of those trails led to **previously undiscovered sites**, such as caves or unnatural clearings.

- In 3 cases, **those same trails later vanished completely**, both physically and digitally.

Most disturbing? Some of the trails **shift position**.

In 2017, a wildlife camera stationed on a fixed tree mount captured a well-worn trail used by caribou. The path was clear. Obvious. Unmistakable.
Six weeks later, the footage shows the animals **veering left**, walking where there had previously been thick brush.
No new clearing was visible — but the old trail?
Gone.

Local guides speak of "ghost roads" — places where the land itself decides whether or not to show you a way forward. The Dene term *Det'ah ghąindeh* loosely translates to "The Way That Wanders When Watched."

One elder explains:

"The land doesn't like being mapped. Some trails are real only when you don't need them. If you go looking for them, they go looking for somewhere else."

A former ranger once tried to retrace a mystery path he and his partner had found leading off Glacier Lake. When he returned with a team the next week, the trail was **still there — but wrong.**
Curved where it had been straight.
Leading uphill when it had previously gone flat.
The ending fork? **Missing.**

His final note:

"I'm not sure if the trail moved… or if I've been moved and the trail didn't follow."

Chapter 49 – The Trees That Don't Fall the Right Way

In a place like Nahanni, trees fall. It's part of the cycle — wind, rot, fire, decay. It's normal.

But what's not normal is **when they fall against the wind**.
Or all in one direction — regardless of slope.
Or when a tree topples… and there's **no damage** where it lands.
Or when the tree is gone the next day.

Across nearly a century of documented activity in the valley, there are dozens of reports where **fallen trees seemed to defy logic**. Reports from forestry agents show trees collapsed **uphill**, away from prevailing winds, or across canyons with no evidence of how they cleared the span.

In 1942, an early park maintenance crew cleared a dozen birches blocking the Goat Plateau access trail. They marked each one for mapping. The next day, returning to log coordinates, they found **six of the felled trees standing again**. Not propped. Not re-planted. **Upright.**

Later inspection showed **new growth rings at the base**. The logs were now **living** trees.

That event was never filed officially. But years later, a retired worker mentioned it in a taped interview:
"The forest gets to decide what's permanent out there. We just visit."

In more recent decades, drone footage and LIDAR scans have picked up **strange fall patterns** — windblown trees scattered **radially** from central points, as if pushed from the inside out. One forestry team compared the arrangement to **blast radii**, but no burn scars were ever found.

In 2008, a team camping along the Flat River woke to find five massive conifers dropped around their tent — perfectly spaced, surrounding them in a loose star pattern.
No wind that night. No weather warning.
No cracking or snapping sounds heard.
Just… silence.

When they checked satellite data from the evening before, the trees had been standing. Clear as day.
Still, no one reported it.
Because how do you file that without sounding insane?

AI analysis revealed over 40 such incidents — referred to by locals as "unnatural treefall" — spread across the Nahanni watershed. In at least 18 of those, multiple trees had clearly fallen, but

with no damage to undergrowth. Moss remained undisturbed. Insect trails across the trunks remained **uncut**, as if the tree had always lain there.

But not all fallen trees stay that way.

Multiple long-time rangers tell stories of trails blocked one day, then open the next. Logs that vanish between shifts. Branches that shift orientation **without disturbance**.
One even claimed to follow what he thought was a logging trail — until he realized **each fallen tree pointed toward him.**

The Dene language has a phrase for this phenomenon: *"Nàhgąh tł'eh"* — "The trees that don't agree with falling."

According to one elder:

"A tree that falls the wrong way isn't confused. It's been told something. And you're not supposed to know what."

And that seems to be the pattern.
In Nahanni, the forest doesn't follow natural rules.
It follows **memory**, or **will**, or maybe **something older than either**.

Because when trees fall, they usually say *a storm passed through*.
But here… it feels more like the storm is waiting to return.

Chapter 50 – The Day the Compass Pointed Up

In every wilderness, there are places where compasses stutter — caught between old ore deposits and ancient magnetic veins. But what happened on the ridge just west of Mount Nirvana wasn't a stutter. It was an **accusation**.

In 2012, a wildlife research team out of Whitehorse set up a high-altitude camp to collect long-term soil samples. The work was standard: map the terrain, log temperature variance, collect lichen and moss. But when they checked their location against the topo-grid and GPS, something didn't make sense.

The camp's coordinates hadn't shifted, but every analog compass they checked — three different brands, one unboxed new that day — didn't just drift east or west. The needles **pointed vertically.** Upward. Not magnetic north. Not to each other. But up.

As if the source of magnetic north had relocated to the sky.

They photographed it. Documented it. But nothing showed in the magnetic data sweep — just blankness. Flatline.

Three hours later, the needles were back to normal.

The AI cross-referenced that timestamp with solar activity, satellite telemetry, and atmospheric ionospheric disturbances. Nothing abnormal. But a separate correlation appeared: **a disappearance** had been logged in that region just one day prior — a solo cartographer who had been **mapping magnetic field lines**.

He had been tracing an anomaly in the valley's rock that seemed to pull instruments off-course. He never filed his last set of coordinates. His field notes ended mid-sentence.

That wasn't the only case.

Back in 1979, two geologists attempted to survey a stone basin northeast of Tungsten Camp. Their notes claim the magnetometer started "reading negative elevation" — as if it was sinking. A week later, they abandoned the study when their GPS (new tech at the time) showed their **altitude as 27 meters below sea level** — on a ridge 2,000 feet up.

They returned with a military-issued device. It read "ERROR."

They were told to classify the data as inconclusive.

Among the 34 records the AI flagged regarding "vertical compass error" or "magnetic inversion," 13 occurred in a tight three-kilometer band around the same glacial rise. Five involved symptoms of vertigo or nausea. Two involved reported dreams of **falling upward**.

The Dene term *"T'áh betsoh gots'įį́"* roughly means "Sky's Mouth." Elders say it is **not a place to be beneath.** When asked to clarify, one man simply said:

"When the earth forgets where it is… the people are not welcome there."

And he would not return.

In the Nahanni, where maps shift and trees don't fall right, even gravity seems optional. But this was different. Not a storm. Not a trick. Not a flare in the magnetosphere.

The compasses knew something had changed.
And for a few hours, they told the truth no one could accept:

That north… wasn't where we left it.

Chapter 51 – The Whisper Caves

Some caves echo.
Others absorb sound completely.
But only a few ever seem to **talk back**.

In the southern reaches of the Nahanni — past the Flat River's bend and beneath an overhang locals call "The Folded Sky" — lies a limestone cave system that's **never been fully mapped**. Not because it's inaccessible, but because something **always interferes.**

Climbing logs from the 1960s refer to the cave mouth as *"Dead Echo Hollow"* — a place where voices **don't bounce**, no matter how loud. And yet, as early as 1923, Dene travelers avoided the area, referring to it as *"Yehgo kí,"* meaning **"the cave that speaks low."**

Over the decades, researchers and hikers alike have described **soft whispers** inside the deeper chambers. Not rushing air. Not dripping water. Not their own breath. But **language** — right on the edge of comprehension. Sometimes a single word. Sometimes a **two-voice conversation**, unintelligible but persistent.

In 2004, a team from the University of Alberta ran audio capture experiments inside the Folded Sky network. One recording captured a steady tone — low, rhythmic, almost like breath. On playback, spectral analysis showed no consistent waveform… but something else stood out:

The sound was only audible between 41.2°F and 43.6°F.
When the cave cooled or warmed slightly, the audio vanished.

In 2011, a documentary crew attempted to film inside the same caves. Their lights failed — twice. Their final recording before abandoning the project contained a 7-second segment where **a woman's voice clearly whispers**:

"It's already been said."

There were no women in the crew.

The AI categorized 22 instances of "sub-audible cave phenomena" in Nahanni's records. 9 included sleep disturbances after exposure. 4 included written notes from team members describing dreams in **languages they didn't speak**.

One hiker wrote:

"It wasn't just noise. I understood what they meant. And when I came out, I forgot the words, but not how they made me feel. Guilty. Like I'd heard something I shouldn't have."

Dene stories hold that the caves are not entrances, but **reservoirs** — not of water or wind, but of **memory**. Some believe the valley stores **every sound ever made within it**, and sometimes, it plays them back.

When asked if the whispers were spirits, one elder said:

"Spirits don't repeat themselves. These do."

And maybe that's the strangest part.
Not that the caves whisper.
But that **some people whisper back.**

Chapter 52 – The Camps That Were Too New

Most disappearances leave behind ruins.
Ashes. Tattered tents. Equipment slowly being consumed by the wilderness.
But Nahanni has a different kind of residue — **too clean, too recent, too unclaimed.**

In 1996, two rangers hiking near Rabbitkettle Lake came across a ridge clearing where a tent was pitched, smoke still rising from a fire ring. Boots by the flap. Two mugs. One half-full of still-warm tea.
They called out.
No answer.

They approached slowly. No wildlife. No wind.
Inside: sleeping bags — zipped and empty. A satellite phone, functional. A GPS unit with one logged location: *you are here*.
But no names. No ID.
No one ever came to retrieve it.
When they returned a day later with a second team… **the camp was gone.**

Not looted. Not packed up.
Gone. As if it hadn't been there.

This wasn't an isolated event.

The AI found 17 separate reports — from 1947 to 2021 — of **camps discovered in immaculate condition**, often with brand-new gear, modern packaging, and in some cases, even **tags still attached**. In every instance:

- **No hiker or permit** matched the equipment.

- **The fire was warm**, sometimes smoldering.

- **There were no approach or departure footprints.**

- Within 48 hours, if not claimed, **the site would vanish**.

One 1983 case involved a forestry pilot who spotted a red canvas tent deep in a ravine inaccessible by foot. He marked the coordinates and flew back with a ground team.
The site was unreachable.

Three days later, a different pilot flew over — **and saw nothing.**
Not even a clearing.

In 2015, a cryptid researcher uploaded trail cam footage of a fresh camp **setting itself** — tent snapping into shape, tarp rising without wind. No visible person.
The footage was removed within 48 hours.
When pressed, he claimed the file corrupted and he "never wanted to talk about that valley again."

Some suspect these are **resets** — temporal loops, displaced camps from previous decades, or **echoes of expeditions that never returned**. Others whisper of *"mirror camps"* — false safe zones designed to lure. Like Venus flytraps for the curious.

Dene lore references **"The Borrowed Fire"** — mysterious flames seen flickering in the woods, where those who approached "never needed to light their own."

When asked if such places were traps, one elder simply nodded:

"If the fire is waiting for you... ask what it had to burn to stay lit."

Whatever these camps are, they raise more than questions.
They raise the possibility that some disappearances in Nahanni don't end with screams, but with comfort.
A fire.
A sleeping bag.
And something waiting just beyond the treeline... that never made a sound.

Chapter 53 – The Ones Who Slept Too Long

Sleep is supposed to restore you.
But in Nahanni, it might **take something instead.**

The first account comes from a 1948 fur trapper's journal, discovered in a rotted lean-to east of Deadmen Valley. He described bedding down after a storm, noting the cold and low visibility. His next entry — dated five days later in a different hand — reads:

"I woke up and the meat was spoiled. The snow was gone. I don't remember going to sleep."

Beside the journal lay a rusted rifle, unfired.
No animals approached the camp.
His supplies were untouched — **except for the lantern**, which was still warm.

In 1974, a geologist named Callum Rourke was reported missing for three days. When search teams found him, he was lying in his tent — heart rate slow, dehydrated, **but otherwise unharmed**. He believed he had only taken a nap.

His last logged note read:

"Lay down at 3:41 p.m. because the trees seemed too loud."

When questioned, he recalled nothing unusual — but aged colleagues swore he looked **five years older**.

The AI flagged 11 such cases from Nahanni Valley alone, plus 6 from adjacent wilderness regions. All involved the following similarities:

- Total sleep duration between **39 and 96 hours**.
- No signs of trauma or drug ingestion.
- The subject always slept **alone**, even in group settings.
- Some subjects were **not aware any time had passed.**

One chilling pattern emerged: many of these "over-sleepers" had previously joked about the valley's **"dead air"** or described feeling as though something was **"pressing the mind to quiet."**

In 2009, a bush pilot dropped off a solo documentarian. She was supposed to check in via sat beacon every 24 hours. On day four, she activated her beacon. When rescued, she claimed she had only spent **a single night**.

But her trail cam showed no activity for three full days.
No movement.
No breathing.
She lay still in her bag, eyes half-open, as if **waiting**.

She later said:

"I wasn't asleep. I just couldn't move because I thought I'd miss something."

In Dene traditions, there are stories of **"long dreamers"** — individuals who fall into a suspended state after venturing too far from sacred ground. It's not coma. It's not sleep. It's a kind of **waiting**.

When asked how they return, one elder shrugged:

"Some don't. Some wake with words in their head that never belonged to them."

One researcher theorized that Nahanni's unique mineral profile and geomagnetic irregularities could induce time distortion — micro sleep turned macro lapse. But that doesn't explain the **photos**, the **camera data**, or why some people wake looking older... while others return **younger**.

In one forgotten SAR memo from 1991:

"Subject found 76 hours post-disappearance. Clothes unchanged. Body temp slightly below baseline. Pupils fixed, but responsive. When woken, subject asked:
'Is it still winter?'
We were in July."

Chapter 54 – When the Radios Played Back Their Own Words

Radios fail.
Batteries die. Signals bounce. Static isn't a mystery — it's part of the terrain.
But Nahanni's static sometimes comes with… **company.**

In 1988, two search-and-rescue volunteers reported hearing their own voices played back to them on UHF band 446.1 — **exactly 27 minutes** after they first spoke.
The transmission came through crystal clear. Identical cadence. Breathing. Even the same moment of laughter at a joke.

But by then, they'd **stopped transmitting**.

The repeat played through only once.
The signal strength showed **no source**.
Their unit wasn't recording.
No relay station in range could explain it.

One of them vomited.

This is not an isolated case.

The AI surfaced 23 separate incidents spanning 1954 to 2022 where handheld or backpack radios in the Nahanni relayed speech patterns that either:

- Matched the user's **own words spoken minutes or hours earlier**,

- Repeated **unspoken thoughts**, according to the user,

- Or contained **unidentified voices** that referenced location-specific elements the speaker had not yet encountered.

In 2006, a team documenting boreal wolf patterns transmitted routine field data. At 7:13 p.m., a technician keyed in coordinates and a description of terrain. At 7:21 p.m., their secondary radio (powered off at the time) emitted the same message — **word for word**, down to an audible throat clear — but the sender's mouth **hadn't moved**.

Witnesses described the moment as **"like hearing your own thoughts spoken back at you by the forest."**

One wilderness medic reported hearing **his dead father's voice** giving medical instructions he hadn't used in decades.
He quit the next day.

In 1975, a mining contractor said the radios in his camp began repeating a woman's voice whispering **"You shouldn't stay here"** — despite no women being in the area. The voice continued for 48 hours at seemingly random intervals before falling silent.

They evacuated.

Some rangers developed their own slang:

- *"Ghost Channel"* – a frequency that would play back field check-ins hours later, often distorted or subtly altered.

- *"Echo Tongue"* – transmissions that were not in English, Dene, or French, yet sounded vaguely familiar. One linguist noted fragments resembled **pre-contact proto-Athabaskan**, a language no one alive should speak.

One audio technician left a chilling note in the margin of his field manual:

"The radios are hearing us before we speak."

Dene elders avoid discussing radio anomalies directly, but one translated phrase was offered:
"Words said near the valley are like stones thrown into still water. The ripples return when you least expect, and not always in the same voice."

Some believe it's a magnetic quirk. Others think the valley functions like an enormous **memory field** — bouncing thoughts, words, even moments, across time.

But some are sure of one thing:

If you hear yourself speaking…
And you're not speaking…
Don't answer.

Chapter 55 – The Ridge Where Drones Fail

It began as an irritation.
A ruined survey.
A lost drone.

But after a dozen failures, a pattern emerged — centered on an unnamed ridgeline northeast of Glacier Lake, where UAVs sent into the airspace above a tree-choked slope either **never returned**, or returned with **footage from somewhere else.**

Early incidents were chalked up to signal loss, harsh thermals, or operator error. But then came 2013, when a Parks Canada team attempted to scan erosion patterns over a 600-meter rise unofficially known as "**Blind Ridge.**"

The first drone vanished at 84 meters altitude — signal lost, telemetry scrambled, no recovery.

The second drone, launched an hour later with a fixed path, returned **on schedule**. But its SD card contained 17 minutes of footage of a different treeline — one with **buildings.**
Old buildings.
Collapsed cabins. Not visible from any adjacent peak.
No coordinates were recorded in the file's metadata.
The drone had no GPS fault. The card had no corruption.

They hiked out to the location, expecting ruins.

There were none.

Another mission in 2016 ended with a recovered drone that had logged coordinates **31 kilometers off course** — across terrain it could not have physically traversed. The battery life alone made it impossible. Yet the barometric data **matched Blind Ridge.**

A private cryptid researcher uploaded a video in 2019 claiming to capture movement in the canopy along the ridge's north slope. The footage was compelling — branches swaying, large shadows between trees. But the drone log showed **no camera activation** during that timestamp.

The drone had been recording from inside its own **carrying case.**

The AI flagged **12 drone anomalies** from that sector alone:

- 6 were unrecovered.

- 4 returned with footage that **could not be mapped**.

- 2 came back with footage that **had already been recorded weeks earlier** — by **different drones**, on **different missions.**

It's as if the valley's airspace doesn't just resist being observed — it **replays old observations**, or **substitutes them.**

The Dene have an expression for it: *"Bet'ahgąį yegha"* — "The place that changes its sky."

A respected hunter who accompanied a drone launch team in 2021 refused to watch the footage after hearing the drone whine stop early.

He only said:

"The birds won't go over it. You shouldn't either."

Wildlife patterns corroborate that. Migratory lines kink sharply **away** from the ridge. No known nests, even among resilient species like ravens. Camera traps reveal silence — days and nights with **zero movement**.

It's not just interference.
It's not just topography.
Something along that ridge doesn't just swallow signal — it **replaces it**.

And if your drone comes back at all…
you should ask **whose eyes it borrowed** while it was gone.

Chapter 56 – The Skeletons That Didn't Belong to Anything

Most remains found in the wild can be identified.
Even when degraded, they tell a story — of age, species, trauma, or disease.
But in the Nahanni… some bones tell **no story at all.**

The first known case appears in a 1921 report from a federal geological expedition. Camped just west of Funeral Range, the team stumbled upon what they believed to be a **human leg bone**, weathered but intact.
Nearby, in a dry wash, they found **a partial jaw with tusk-like projections** — curved inward, not outward. The team assumed it was caribou or perhaps malformed bear remains. But one physician on-site made a note:

"The foramen is inconsistent with known regional fauna. The dentition is… wrong. Too human. And yet not."

No samples were preserved. The bones were left behind — and when another team returned weeks later, they were gone.

Over the decades, other reports followed.

In 1957, a pair of hikers near the Headless Range found what they thought was a bear skeleton, until they noticed the skull lacked **a defined snout**, and the limb structure supported **bipedal weight distribution.**
The femur was over 19 inches long.
They took photos. None survived. The negatives were reportedly "accidentally fogged."

In 1982, a Royal Canadian Mounted Police forensics technician was flown in to examine a partial ribcage unearthed by landslide runoff. His brief notes describe a thoracic structure similar to a primate but with **bone porosity akin to deep-sea mammals.**
The bones were stored at a temporary station outside Nahanni Butte.
A week later, the station burned down. The case was never re-opened.

According to the AI synthesis of expedition notes, unarchived logs, and indirect witness statements, at least **nine distinct findings** across a century may involve:

- **Non-human primate traits**, including abnormal arm-to-leg ratios.

- **Dental structures inconsistent with carnivores or herbivores.**

- In some cases, **hollow or semi-hollow bones** with internal pitting — a trait found only in high-altitude birds.

Several specimens reportedly turned **cold to the touch**, even after being stored indoors. One trapper described the bones as "cold like glacier rock, even in firelight."

In recent years, more skeletal finds have surfaced — quietly.
Anonymous photos sent to cryptid researchers.
X-rays leaked from field hospitals.
Sketches from amateur archaeologists showing skull shapes with **double occipital ridges.**

None of these were ever confirmed. But one photo, sent by a bush pilot in 2016, shows a partial pelvis lodged between rocks — twisted, warped, yet **undeniably bipedal.**

No universities responded to inquiries.
No one claimed the image.
The pilot disappeared two months later.

Traditional Dene stories speak of creatures who **"buried their own bones,"** returning to retrieve them **"so we would not know their shape."** Elders warn that to find such remains is not luck — it's warning.

"Their dead don't stay where they fall. The valley does not keep what it cannot explain."

Whatever these skeletons once were, they were not supposed to be found.
And they may not be done **being something**.

Chapter 57 – The Ice That Burned

Snow burns.
Everyone knows this — frostbite, wind exposure, ice pressed too long against bare skin.
But the Nahanni has a kind of cold that burns before it touches you.

In 1973, two graduate students on a hydrology survey near the Ram Plateau documented what they believed was a seasonal spring emerging from glacial ice. The runoff tested clean — near-pure melt, no contaminants. But when one of them slipped while stepping near the trickle, his wrist submerged for less than two seconds.

Within 30 minutes, blisters began to form.
Within two hours, the skin had split.
The wound presented **as a burn**, not frostbite.
Ambient temperature at the time was **42°F.**

Their final report noted the injury as "thermic lesion of unknown origin."

The AI analysis uncovered **14 total incidents** (between 1951 and 2019) where skin contact with snowbanks, ice layers, or "cold mist" resulted in:

- Blistering, similar to second-degree burns.

- Nerve sensitivity and numbness lasting weeks.

- Surface tissue damage inconsistent with temperature exposure.

One 1991 field medic wrote:

"The hand looks like it was dipped in acid — red, wet, glossy. But it was snow he touched. Nothing else."

In 2008, a hiker collapsed after kneeling on a frozen patch beneath a waterfall east of Deadmen Valley. She described the ice as "humming" beneath her, and said her skin "felt like it had caught fire."
Her knees bore burn-like lesions — later confirmed to be **electrothermal in appearance**, though no current source was found nearby.

Some of these incidents coincided with **auroral activity**, but not all.
Others occurred during absolute silence, in shaded ravines, under overcast skies.

One drone-captured thermal overlay showed a curious pattern: a consistent **heat trace** beneath a line of permafrost — **as if something warm were moving beneath it**, creating short-lived thermal pockets that quickly froze over again. When a team attempted to chip into the same location 24 hours later, the patch had solidified to an unnaturally hard state.

The working theory from one retired geologist: **frictional layering** caused by extreme pressure variances under the valley's fault zones. Another theory involves **unknown ion exchange** from subterranean metals. But those theories don't explain:

- Why only **some** patches of ice react this way.

- Why no metallic residue is left behind.

- Why the burns sometimes appear **before** direct contact.

One Dene elder offered a quieter explanation.

"Some places remember the fire that was there before the ice."

The stories speak of hot rivers that once steamed from the valley's bones — rivers that were **"quieted by snow, but not forgotten."** They say some ice still **"burns with old blood."**

If true, this isn't just permafrost.
It's memory frozen into the land.
And sometimes, it remembers how to hurt you.

Chapter 58 – The Season That Loops

The mind forgets details.
Memory softens the edges.
But what if the forest doesn't?

In the spring of 1999, a veteran wildlife photographer returned to the same moss-covered bend in the Flat River where he had filmed moose the previous autumn. He knew the trail. Knew the trees. Knew the bend by heart.

And it was exactly the same.

The same fallen spruce still lay across the stones — bark flaking the same way.
The same birdcall patterns echoed across the water, timed to the second from his old footage.
The clouds overhead matched his stills.
When he compared the images… even the **leaf curl** on the edge of a birch was **identical.**

He packed up and flew out the next day, shaken.

In 2007, a botanist surveying lichen growth reported that her markers — placed five weeks earlier — were untouched, as though time had frozen. She re-recorded light levels and humidity.
Same as before.
Same cloud cover.
Same insect population.
Her team re-ran the data.
It matched the previous survey line **bit for bit**.

They laughed it off. Until the same thing happened again the next year.

The AI logged **11 independent field notes** referring to time-looped conditions in the Nahanni — all from different professions, eras, and sectors of the valley. Five described weather patterns "repeating." Three involved GPS tracks that **recreated identical paths**, even when hikers attempted to deviate. Two described sensory déjà vu so intense it caused panic attacks.

But one case stood out.

In 1981, a solo cartographer named Roland C. Finch disappeared for six days while attempting to chart an unnamed ridge southeast of Deadmen Valley. When he returned, sunburned and disoriented, he claimed he had been stuck in **"the same afternoon"** — clouds above unmoving, a breeze that never stopped, and birds that called the same five notes… **over and over.**

His boots showed minimal wear.
His gear was untouched.
But his beard had grown six days longer.
He had aged — but his **environment hadn't.**

In Dene teachings, there is mention of **"Dígha tǫchǫ́"** — "The place that has not chosen a time." They say some places never agreed to move forward like the rest of the world. That if you step into them, the world might forget you… or wait for you… or make you **repeat yourself** until you are no longer yourself.

One elder said:

"You won't notice at first. The path seems familiar because you walked it before. Then it seems familiar because you're walking it again. And again. And again."

He smiled grimly.

"If the birds are always calling the same way, go back. If the light is always behind you, go back. And if your footsteps are already there…
you were not the first you to walk them."

Chapter 59 – The Campfires Already Burning

Campfires mean life.
Warmth. Safety. Company.
But in Nahanni, the glow of a fire in the dark might mean **you were expected.**

In 2002, two seasoned hunters crested a low ridge just before dusk and saw the unmistakable flicker of firelight through the black spruce below. They had been walking for six hours and hadn't seen a soul. No tracks. No prints. No smoke trail earlier that day.

Still, the fire was there. Orange. Steady. Inviting.

By the time they descended into the clearing, **the light was gone.**
Not extinguished — **gone.**
No ashes. No logs. No disturbed ground.
Just silence.

Later that night, as they made camp further up the slope, one of them spotted a dim glow again — this time **closer.**
They didn't investigate.

This pattern repeats.

A Parks Canada report from 1985 notes a fire observed from a surveillance aircraft over the upper Ram River. Coordinates were marked. Rangers dispatched. When they arrived 14 hours later, the fire was still visible from a distance — smoke curling just above the tree line.

When they entered the site:

- No heat.

- No fire ring.

- No tools or signs of human presence.
  Just a circle of **warmed soil.**

The AI analysis surfaced **19 recorded instances** of unexplained firelight phenomena between 1938 and 2020:

- 7 involved firelight seen where no known camps existed.

- 4 involved **cleared spaces** that suggested recent human activity — without occupants.

- 3 involved campfires found **actively burning** with no sign of ignition tools, fuel stores, or footprints.

- 2 involved observers who saw **their own gear** waiting at the site.

In one 1999 incident, a solo hiker documented finding a fire — burning low in a circle of stones — beside a tent that was an **identical model** to his own. He approached slowly, calling out.
No response.
Inside the tent: a sleeping bag — **same brand, same color** — unzipped.

He left.
Didn't take photos.
Didn't sleep for the rest of the trip.

Traditional Dene stories describe **"the fires that arrive first"** — flames that "light where no hand has struck flint," often in areas that would become the site of tragedy or loss.
These fires are said to be **warnings**, or worse: **invitations.**

One elder warned:

"When you see a fire that's already waiting for you… it doesn't want to share warmth.
It wants to see if you remember how it ends."

Whatever they are, these campfires don't appear to be illusions.
They warm the ground.
They flicker through binoculars.
Sometimes, they **respond to being watched** — growing brighter or dimmer.

But if you step close…
you may find the fire was waiting for someone just like you.
Maybe it still is.

Chapter 60 – The Hills That Hum at Dusk

Some wilderness sounds are predictable.
Birdsong before dawn. Wind in the treetops.
But Nahanni has hills that don't echo. They **hum.**

The phenomenon begins at dusk.

In 1977, a team of three field biologists set camp along a slope west of the Funeral Range. As the sun dipped behind the trees, they reported a rising pressure in their ears, followed by a low **pulsing tone**—like standing beside a diesel engine buried beneath stone.

They dismantled and checked their gear. No power sources. No batteries overheating.
The hum persisted for 41 minutes.

The sound stopped exactly when the final ray of sun left the ridge.

They slept with earplugs the rest of the trip.

In 1992, a solo cartographer recorded a sound file while camping near a ridgeline known locally as "*Crow Spine*." The tone begins at 7:46 p.m. and increases in volume for 12 minutes before tapering off.
Spectrographic analysis shows a consistent **28.9 Hz frequency** with modulation pulses.
When researchers tried to replicate the hum, they couldn't—there were **no manmade sources** or geological patterns to match.

The AI aggregated **29 separate field references** to "evening hums" or "twilight droning" in the Nahanni, most concentrated in three locations:

- The **northwestern basin** near Flat River bends.

- A **saddle-shaped ridge** near Glacier Lake.

- The **eastern edge** of Deadmen Valley.

Common elements:

- **Begins at twilight**, lasts between 9 and 44 minutes.

- **Cannot be recorded** clearly on standard audio equipment (in 13 of 17 attempts).

- Some report **physical effects**: dizziness, jaw pain, nausea, or nosebleeds.

- Animals **vacate** the area before the hum begins.

In one documented case, two hikers attempted to crest a humming hill after dark. They reported a rising vibration in their boots, followed by a sharp pressure "like being underwater." One blacked out. The other described it as "a whisper inside your bones."

When they reached the top, everything was silent.
But their watches were **42 minutes off from each other.**
One had lost time.
One had gained it.

Dene oral tradition includes reference to *"The Stones That Breathe"* — sacred hills where the land was said to **exhale warning** as light left the sky. These areas were avoided not because of danger… but because **they weren't meant to be entered** at certain hours.

A 2018 SAR radio operator wrote:

"We don't transmit when the humming starts. You'll miss the callouts anyway.
It's like the ground is louder than your own voice."

Is it seismic?
Subterranean gas movement?
Ancient geothermal echo?

Maybe.
Or maybe the land is doing exactly what it's always done — **responding to who's walking on it.**

When the hills hum at dusk, they don't make music.
They send a message.
And some messages are not meant for us.

Chapter 61 – The Ones Who Watched from the Trees

They were never photographed. Rarely spoken of. And always seen from just beyond the firelight. The Nahanni Valley holds many secrets, but few stir such immediate instinct as the accounts of something watching — large, silent, unseen but felt. For over a century, stories have circulated of figures in the timberline, towering and still, with shoulders too broad and eyes that reflect light too close to the ground. It's easy to dismiss as fear. Easy to say it's bear-shadow or imagination. But the patterns… they keep surfacing. And they don't align with anything else.

In 1914, trapper William Collins wrote in his logbook that he awoke to "cracking from the willows" and spotted "a tall figure — not bear — watching the camp." It didn't run when spotted. It just turned. And walked away on two legs. He never set another trap in Nahanni.

In 1928, a German prospector named Karl Fleischman went missing near Glacier Lake. When his partner was found weeks later, dehydrated and shaking, he told officials that something big had been "circling the tents at night," throwing rocks and snapping branches — but never showing itself. "It wanted us to know we were being allowed," he muttered in broken English. "Allowed to stay. But not to build." His hands had deep scratch marks — defensive. Not from claws, but fingers.

Historical survey records and modern expedition logs show over a dozen mentions of tracks found in mud, snow, or even lichen-covered granite, with no clear entry or exit point. Most described: Bipedal stride. Over 16 inches long. No arch or heel structure consistent with known mammals. One forestry worker near Deadmen Valley photographed a line of prints in early spring — over compact snowpack, with no other tracks anywhere nearby. He hiked five kilometers back to the same ridge a week later. The prints were still there. Untouched.

Multiple hikers have reported a "watched" sensation that came on suddenly — as if the entire forest stopped moving. Birdsong halts. Wind drops. The air thickens. In 2004, a group of geology students pitched camp near a mineral exposure south of Prairie Creek. Around 2 a.m., one student reported hearing a slow exhale right outside her tent. She unzipped the flap. Nothing. But in the morning, there were two indentations in the moss — large, flat, symmetrical — less than five feet from her head. She didn't finish the field course.

Careful pattern analysis of reported sightings, expedition logs, and flight path anomalies reveals unusual overlap between these observations and: geothermal venting zones, known electromagnetic disturbance areas, and silence pockets where recording equipment fails to pick up ambient sounds. These sightings are not random. They cluster in precise areas, often marked in local oral maps as places not to linger. Even modern drones have failed near these zones — some returning with corrupted footage, others simply going dark.

In 2019, a field operator retrieved five seconds of footage showing a tall, bipedal shape moving through misted trees. The file also contained audio… of the operator's voice. A phrase he swears he never spoke: "You weren't supposed to see this." He hadn't used the mic. He was alone.

In Dene tradition, the creatures are called *Na'ats'ehch'aa* — not "wildmen," but more precisely: the brother whose trail we don't follow. They are not feared. They are respected — and avoided. "They are not gone," said one elder in Fort Liard. "They are waiting for us to forget they were ever common." He described a tale of a man who built shelter on a warm ridge where no animals nested. Weeks later, he was found asleep in his tent — eyes open, body untouched. His boots were neatly placed by the flap. A line of giant, bare footprints led away from the camp and vanished at the river.

Those who return to the same site twice — armed with cameras, scanners, or instruments — report strange behavior: Disorientation. Temporal distortion. Exact repetition of previous events. One biologist described seeing the same shadow figure, at the same time of day, on two consecutive trips — years apart. "It's like they pressed play again," she said. "As if I hadn't left. As if the moment… was still waiting."

Whatever these beings are — they've seen us before we see them. And in the Nahanni, that may be the only warning you'll ever get. The second comes when they decide whether you're worth seeing again.

Chapter 62 – The Creatures That Shouldn't Still Be Here

The land keeps its secrets.
But sometimes, it also **preserves them**.

The Nahanni Valley's remote geography, hidden geothermal activity, and long oral history of "things that don't belong" has fueled reports for over a century of creatures that, by all scientific reasoning, should not exist anymore. Yet, the same legends persist — not just through storytelling, but through **physical encounters, unexplained remains, and environmental irregularities**.

This chapter is about the ones that don't fit even in cryptozoology.
The creatures that seem **left behind**… or somehow **protected**.

The Mammoths That Walk in Mist

In 1899, fur traders along the Flat River reported hearing **trumpet-like vocalizations** from across thick fog near a warm spring valley. In the snow: **tracks shaped like giant round pads with claws**, spaced too far apart for elk or moose. They abandoned their trapline.

In 1943, a Royal Canadian Air Force pilot conducting a survey flight north of Glacier Lake allegedly saw a **massive grey creature** moving slowly through low trees on a snowless patch of ground. The crew filed a report stating it had a "shaggy silhouette, a large back hump, and curled tusk-like projections."

More than one trapper in the 1950s recounted stories of hearing **"deep thuds"** and low growling echoing through canyons during mild winters — always in areas with geothermal ground where **vegetation bloomed oddly out of season.**

Some Dene elders refer to "the last wool bear," a creature that roams the southern valleys only when winter refuses to arrive. One elder claimed, "If the trees still bend, it still walks."

Wolves That Are Too Large, and Too Quiet

In multiple accounts dating back to the early 1900s, especially during the **Deadmen Valley disappearances,** there were reports of wolves "the size of ponies" seen from a distance — but without the usual behavioral traits. They moved in **total silence**, never howled, and **left no scat, no scent**.

Modern hunters (two cases from the 1980s and 2011) described **pale, ash-grey wolves** with massive heads and strangely **sloped backs**, unlike any known canid profile. In one case, a freshly killed caribou carcass was found **dragged against the river current**, teeth marks measured at 5.3 inches wide.

One photo, reportedly taken by a bush pilot in 1994, appears to show a **wolf-like shape with unusually thick forearms**, standing on a rocky outcrop above a steaming snowless slope. The photo was allegedly confiscated after it was submitted to a local wildlife office. No copy remains.

The Maned Bears of Nahanni

One of the most enduring — and feared — legends is that of the **Maned Bear**, a cryptid reported during both indigenous oral tradition and European expeditions. Described as **larger than grizzlies**, these creatures have a **dark mane** running from the shoulders down the back, and an **unusual forward-canted gait**.

Several early prospectors from the 1930s onward claimed to have encountered these creatures or their remains — one report mentions **scored bones** and "smoothed rocks" inside an old cave, as if the bear had nested, or stored food.

A man in 1987 claimed to have seen one "rise from the snowpack like a rock that unfolded." He noted it had **yellowed eyes** and moved downhill without losing its upright posture. He left Nahanni by air the next morning and never returned.

Geothermal Pockets and Anomalous Life

What connects many of these encounters is the **presence of warm ground, steam vents, or persistent plant growth**, even in mid-winter conditions.

Satellite images in 2013 identified over a dozen zones within the Nahanni reserve that show **thermal retention inconsistent with latitude and altitude**. Many of the cryptid sightings occur within or adjacent to these regions.

Several surveys in the 1960s attempted to chart these warm anomalies — but results were either "inconclusive" or "lost" according to government archives.

Possibility or Projection?

Scientists have long speculated that Pleistocene holdouts may have existed into recorded history — isolated, microclimate-preserved creatures surviving in places we cannot reach. In most of the world, that's pure theory.

But Nahanni isn't most of the world.

Its valleys form a basin where **movement is limited**, and **escape is controlled** by terrain. Glacial runoff, geothermal bubbles, and permafrost fractures create **echo chambers of preserved life** — both in sediment, and possibly, in flesh.

They shouldn't be here.
And yet the stories have never gone away.

If it were just a myth, it wouldn't repeat with **geographic consistency**.
If it were all fantasy, there wouldn't be **shifting migration zones** mapped by sound and witness.

They're not the ones out of place.
We are.

Chapter 63 – What the Valley Keeps

You've followed the maps. You've read the reports. You've stood with the missing and sat with the searchers. And now, after sixty-two chapters and a descent through stories both terrifying and tragic, we find ourselves at the edge of the trail — where the path ends, and the valley takes over.

And still, there are no neat conclusions.

This place — the Nahanni — doesn't conform to logic or tidy explanations. It leaves bodies decapitated and untouched gear scattered like breadcrumbs in the moss. It swallows voices, alters directions, changes weather, and sometimes shifts the very terrain beneath your feet. It's not just unexplained — it's uninterested in explaining itself. And that's what makes it different.

Some believe the valley is cursed. Others say it's sacred. Some call it a natural anomaly, where weather, geology, and human fallibility combine into a deadly cocktail. But those who've walked its trails, paddled its rivers, or stared too long into its fog-choked ravines? They know better. They've felt it. The cold that presses in without warning. The forest that listens. The silence that shouldn't be there.

This isn't just a dangerous place — it may be one of the creepiest places on Earth.

The Nahanni doesn't feel empty. It feels occupied — by something you can't quite name. A memory, maybe. A presence. It watches, it waits, and when it chooses to act, it does so without mercy or logic. One step too far, one decision made at the wrong bend in the river, and you're gone. No struggle, no noise, no explanation.

And yet, people keep coming.

They bring drones, LIDAR, GPS units, and optimism. They come with questions about ancient disappearances and stories of glowing eyes, massive tracks, or sounds that rise from the gorge like voices echoing from another time. They carry trail markers and leave voice memos. Some return changed. Some never return at all.

Why? Why keep searching?

Because once you've heard the stories — once you've seen the patterns, the maps, the names lost and found — you understand that this place holds something rare. Something real. Something off. And if you're the kind of person who needs to know, then the Nahanni becomes a magnet.

Not just for mystery, but for something more primal: the need to confront the edge of understanding and peer beyond it.

You won't find closure here. This chapter isn't about resolution. It's about recognition — that some places don't give answers because they were never meant to. They're here to remind us that the world is still wild. That danger doesn't always roar; sometimes, it whispers from the spruce. Sometimes it hums just beneath the soil.

So go ahead — keep looking. Keep asking. But do it with caution, and respect. Bring your gear, your instincts, and your exit plan. And don't forget: some questions, once asked in a place like this, don't ever stop echoing.

The Nahanni doesn't owe us anything.

It never did.

But it keeps the curious coming. And it keeps the creepiest secrets hidden right where they want to be — somewhere between legend and loss.

Just remember this before you go back out there:

Some places keep their secrets.

And some secrets keep the places alive.

Appendix A – Cryptid Encounter Log: Nahanni Non-Hominid Sightings

1899 – Flat River

Cryptid: Woolly Mammoth (theory)
Description: Traders heard trumpet-like sounds echoing from dense fog near a geothermal zone. When they investigated, they discovered massive, rounded tracks with claw impressions. The spacing and scale were inconsistent with any known local fauna. The group abandoned their trapline prematurely and left the area.

1943 – North of Glacier Lake (Air Survey)

Cryptid: Large Shaggy Creature with Tusks
Description: During a reconnaissance flight, an RCAF crew observed a grey, humped creature moving slowly through a snowless clearing. It had long, curved tusk-like features and a lumbering gait. The crew filed an official report, which was never made public.

1950s – Southern Nahanni

Cryptid: Unknown
Description: Multiple trappers and seasonal prospectors reported deep thuds and low growls near snow-free warm valleys, where out-of-season plant growth was observed. Though no sightings were made, the sounds and movement in thick mist suggested a large, ground-moving creature associated with geothermal areas.

1987 – Unnamed Ridge

Cryptid: Maned Bear
Description: A hunter encountered a massive upright creature emerging from a drift of snow. It had yellowed eyes, a thick mane along its shoulders, and moved downhill without falling to all fours. The witness departed the valley by air the next morning and refused to return.

1994 – Steaming Ridge (Aerial Photo)

Cryptid: Dire Wolf (possible)
Description: A bush pilot photographed a large, wolf-shaped silhouette with unusually thick forearms, standing above a geothermal slope. The image was submitted to regional wildlife authorities and was reportedly confiscated. The pilot claimed it was unlike any known species.

2004 – Deadmen Valley

Cryptid: Oversized Wolves
Description: Hunters encountered extremely large, ash-grey wolves. Unlike normal wolves, these made no sound, left no trace or scent, and never howled. One partially eaten caribou carcass was found upstream, against the current, with teeth marks far wider than any known predator.

2013 – Thermal Hot Spot Clusters (Satellite Data)

Cryptid: Unconfirmed
Description: Satellite imaging of the Nahanni Reserve revealed dozens of thermal anomalies — persistent hot spots not aligned with natural topography or seasonal weather. Many known cryptid encounters correspond to these locations, suggesting a possible link between geothermal activity and ecological preservation of prehistoric species or anomalous wildlife behavior.

Appendix B – Master Log of Unexplained Phenomena in the Nahanni Valley

Category: Mysterious Deaths

Phenomenon: Headless Corpses (The McLeod Brothers, Martin Jorgensen, others)

Summary: Between 1908 and 1945, multiple explorers were found decapitated in the valley. Most notably, the McLeod brothers in 1908 were discovered with their heads missing and no signs of struggle. Martin Jorgensen's cabin was burned, and his skeleton found without a skull. No suspects or motives were ever found. Theories range from local revenge to cryptid attack or ancient traps. These incidents are the source of Nahanni's nickname: The Valley of Headless Men.

Category: Disappearances

Phenomenon: Unsolved Vanishings

Summary: Dozens of travelers and researchers have vanished in the Nahanni over the last century. Some left behind tents, gear, and fires still burning. Most never left footprints beyond a few hundred meters. Weather conditions were stable in many cases. Search teams found nothing. Names include Albert Fahlman (1936), prospector Johnson Garrett (1954), and wildlife biologist Susan Hill (2002). Several victims were experienced outdoorsmen with no history of psychological conditions.

Category: Cryptids

Phenomenon: Bigfoot, Mammoths, Dire Wolves, Maned Bears

Summary: Numerous cryptids have been sighted in the region, often associated with geothermal zones. Witnesses describe massive bipedal beings, ancient megafauna-like shapes, and wolves 'too big to be real'. The creatures avoid direct contact and often disappear suddenly. Sightings cluster around Prairie Creek, Flat River fog banks, and thermal clearings south of Deadmen

Valley. Some of these creatures match prehistoric descriptions, prompting theories of ecological time capsules.

Category: Anomalous Zones

Phenomenon: Thermal Vents, Silence Pockets, Disorientation Zones

Summary: Geothermal activity sustains unusual warm zones where plant life thrives in winter. These areas often correspond with silence zones where no animals are heard and navigation equipment fails. Witnesses report loops in time and reappearance at original campsites without directional change. Thermal imaging has confirmed zones that maintain ground temperatures far above the ambient air — unexplained by any known volcanic or seismic activity.

Category: UFOs / Aerial Anomalies

Phenomenon: Lights in the Sky, Interference, Vanishing Objects

Summary: Bright lights, silent flying objects, and electromagnetic interference have been recorded since at least the 1950s. In 1971, an RCMP report described 'a pulsing white object that changed direction without slowing.' Drone footage from 2018 showed unexplained motion blurs in a clear sky — data later corrupted. Pilots avoid some flight paths due to sensor dropouts. Anecdotes include aircraft being "shadowed" by lights they couldn't outrun.

Category: Unnatural Fires

Phenomenon: Fires Preceding Arrivals

Summary: Teams frequently discover campfires already burning upon arrival to remote clearings. Logs show no matches, tools, or ignition sources. Some fires appear warm long after sighting. Several explorers reported hallucinations or voices near these fires. Despite fresh burn evidence, no human tracks are ever found nearby. Some flames reportedly burned in freezing rain.

Category: Sound Anomalies

Phenomenon: Voices, Echoes, Radio Playback

Summary: Voices not tied to known persons have been heard through radios. Replays of earlier speech, whispers outside tents, and harmonics from empty canyons persist in field logs. In 2004, a group recorded their own voices responding before they spoke. Known zones include The Gates, Sunblood Mountain flank, and Fog Hollow. Audio phenomena often coincide with brief equipment failure or compass spin.

Category: Indigenous Lore

Phenomenon: Tribe That Disappeared, Warnings of the Deep Valley

Summary: Dene and Nah?ą Dehé traditions reference a powerful tribe that walked into the valley and was never seen again. Elders speak of warm earth, watchers in the trees, and names that should not be spoken aloud. Warnings include not following fires, never climbing certain ridges, and respecting 'the eyes that wait above the tree line.' Oral history insists the land will test the uninvited and that 'some echoes aren't echoes.'

Category: Visual Anomalies

Phenomenon: Trail Changes, Shifting Landmarks

Summary: Explorers have reported trails that appear on one day and vanish the next. In some areas, satellite imagery shows features inconsistent with on-the-ground views. Mapping the Nahanni repeatedly results in different terrain reports and unexplained gaps. Some coordinates don't match terrain seen during approach flights. Hikers have reported cairns moving overnight and ridgelines not aligning with compass bearings.

Appendix C – Indigenous Lore & Place-Name Interpretations

Nahʔą Dehé (Nahanni Valley)

Meaning 'River of the Land of the Nahʔą', referencing a semi-mythic people who once lived deep in the valley. Local oral tradition describes them as powerful and feared, eventually vanishing without a trace. The valley is considered spiritually significant and dangerous if disrespected. Stories include warnings not to call certain names aloud, and to never approach places the animals refuse to enter.

Deadmen Valley

Named after the discovery of the McLeod brothers' headless bodies. In Dene narratives, it is said to be 'a place the Earth closes around you.' Shamans were once forbidden from traveling here alone. Some say the wind that passes through here carries the names of the dead.

The Gates

Towering canyon walls near the South Nahanni River entrance. Known to local communities as 'the watchers' or 'the doorway you do not return from'. Associated with sightings of shadow figures and whispering wind. It's said once you pass through, 'something watches to see if you leave the right way.'

Sunblood Mountain

So named for its red slopes, Dene accounts describe it as a mountain that bleeds light. Considered the resting place of a spirit that guards the valley. Hikers report disorientation and strange magnetic pulls. Some believe it hides a spirit gate or ancient burial marker.

Flat River

A calm, slow-moving tributary with a dark reputation. Legends say the river is deceptive — 'flat water hides deep stories.' Some believe the current can split into two timelines. Disappearances near Flat River are attributed to spirits reclaiming what was stolen.

Kraus Hot Springs

Thermal springs known for unseasonal warmth. While popular among travelers, Dene elders say 'steam doesn't rise here alone.' Spirits are said to rest beneath the waters. Sudden fog banks and animal silence have been reported. Avoided at dusk or after thunder.

Appendix D – Map of Nahanni